Advance Praise for Declutter Your Life

I absolutely love this easy decluttering and organization guide. I've been in the DIY and home design space for over 25 years and this book is one in a million for those looking to turn their home into a stress-free sanctuary.

Tanya Memme - TV Host/Personality, A&E Network

Maria does a fabulous job of turning the seemingly daunting task of decluttering into a simple, straightforward, and ultimately life-affirming process that yields terrific results both spatially and psychologically. She provides the tools necessary to turn your home into a place that feels as wonderful as it looks!

Loren Ruch - Group SVP, Production & Development, HGTV

This guide is uplifting, creative, and practical! If you are looking to lower your stress and increase your happiness every time you walk into your home, get this book immediately.

Rachael Jayne Groover - Best-selling author of *Powerful and Feminine*

DECLUTTER YOUR HOME

Create Simplicity and Elegance in Your Life

Maria Gavin

DECLUTTER YOUR HOME
Create Simplicity and Elegance in Your Life

Deep Pacific Press
117 E 37th St. #5980
Loveland, CO 80538

Deep
Pacific
Press

For information about special discounts for bulk purchases, please contact:
mariagavin@gavinmail.com

Cover design: Patrick Knowles
Interior design & formatting: Mark Thomas / Coverness.com

ISBN 978-1-956108-15-6
Ebook ISBN 978-1-956108-16-3

Printed in the United States

First Edition

To my wonderful, crazy family. I love you more than I can say.

As I unclutter my life, I free myself to
answer the callings of my soul.

Dr. Wayne Dyer (Thought Leader, Speaker, and Writer)

TABLE OF CONTENTS

PART 1

THE HOME AND THE CASE FOR DECLUTTERING IT

1.

NICE TO MEET YOU

One sunny Los Angeles afternoon in my junior year of high school, I come home to find my mother and sister Cristina, arms crossed, raising their eyebrows at me.

"Really?" they say.

"Huh?"

"We found it."

"Found what?"

"The tray of dirty dishes under your bed."

I was busted. Not surprising. Cleaning up, organizing, and making things pretty were pretty much not in my wheelhouse – or anywhere near it.

So how did an admitted slob go from stashing days' worth of dishes under the bed just to avoid a little housework to a love of decluttering, organizing, and creating beauty in the home? Partly, of course, I grew up. But I also overcame my fear that it would be too difficult and too time-consuming.

I realized it was actually fairly easy to create a home I was proud of

- one that reflected me and my tastes - thanks to a few tips and tricks anyone can learn. And guess what? Surprise, surprise – it could even be fun and creative!

But my most important realization goes back to Dr. Wayne Dyer's words, "As I unclutter my life, I free myself to answer the callings of my soul."

CLUTTER IS A FORM OF STUCK ENERGY

Stuck energy drains us of our ability to focus, to be productive, even to be physically and mentally healthy. It can also make us feel 'blah' - drained of any sense of passion in our lives. Clutter literally blocks our ability to create and live the life we want, in alignment and congruency with what we claim to value - whether that's relationships, family, getting ahead in our careers, taking a class to become a better cook or artist, volunteering, whatever. It can even block our ability to know, define, or articulate what it is that we want.

Aesthetics of Joy founder Ingrid Fetell Lee says (aestheticsofjoy.com):

> A home is...an idea about how we want to live that we are creating in the world. A house feels like home if the physical things in it reflect this idea. But if we don't know how we want to live, no amount of stuff can make it feel homey.

So, if we want to reclaim our focus, creativity, productivity, wellbeing, and passion for life, we need to get serious about creating the *space* for those things, including the space for knowing how it is we want to live and how we want our home to support us in that.

WHO AM I?

Thanks for picking up this book. My name's Maria. Born and raised in Los Angeles, I have spent my professional life as a coordinator, writer, and producer of unscripted television (read nonfiction, documentary, and kinder, gentler reality TV shows). I also teach film and TV production at the college level. So, what am I doing writing a book like this?

INSPIRATION BY ANY OTHER NAME

My late mother's things. My sister's things. Her fiancé's things. My things. Toys, litterboxes, and baskets (the two cats' things). And not enough room for all of it by any stretch of the imagination. Garage. Cabinets. Cupboards. Closets. Shelves. Tables. Counters. Floor space. All of them covered with boxes, papers, clothes, and décor - bursting at the seams and completely unnavigable.

Where was my house?

A place full of beauty, space, and things that make me feel calm and peaceful? Full of things that make me feel at home? Not full of so many *things*.

My mother's death and some quirks of timing meant all of the aforementioned clutter was, in fact, taking up residence – and room – in the house, along with my sister and her fiancé, who I truly love and truly love having around.

But all that stuff!

Something had to give.

As Oscar Wilde supposedly said on his deathbed, "It's either the wallpaper or me. One of us has to go!"

Since I didn't want it to be me, I decided to make some changes to honor my home and make it a sacred place. I took my skills as a documentary writer-producer and did my research.

- I decluttered.
- I cleaned.
- I organized.
- I painted.
- I battle-tested all sorts of tips and tricks and came up with a compendium of what actually works to get you unstuck: a system that can stand you in good stead now and help you and your home grow together into your ever-evolving future.

You're reading it now.

THIS BOOK

This book is a love letter to the idea of home and to organization within the home, which I call "curation," a repeating cycle, much like breathing, of taking in what serves us and letting go of what doesn't. In. Out. In. Out.

Curation creates ease and simplicity in our lives.

Ease and simplicity create beauty and elegance. When I say beauty and elegance, I'm not talking about an art collection, vintage rugs, or your very best china, although those things are lovely and can certainly be part of it.

When scientists and engineers talk about elegance, they mean achieving the maximum desired effect with the least effort. I'm talking about the beauty and elegance that come from paring away the unnecessary, refining the essentials, then adding the little extra touches. A bowl of lemons by the fridge. A shoe rack by the front door. The net bags that save wear and tear on your laundry. The Goldilocks "just right" pillow on your bed – not too full, not too flat.

What I'm talking about is setting up your home in a way that supports you, making your everyday life easier and simpler. Even more than beauty and elegance, ease and simplicity give you *time* - time you can spend with loved ones, engaging in activities you love. Because, ultimately, it's the moments *within* our homes that matter.

THE LAYOUT

Part 1 of this book offers some general thoughts about the home, including clutter, how it affects you, and how to get rid of it.

In Part 2 we'll go room-by-room, with some thoughts on organization and specific ways to make each space more spacious and beautiful. Plus a few tips for when you're *not* home...better known as traveling.

Along the way, I'll offer what I call "Cheap Tricks" and "Elegant Tips" for each area of the house. Finally, there are ideas for creating ease and simplicity in everything from sleep hygiene and bath time to thoughts for when guests come to stay - with their own stuff!

These ideas are meant to be expansive for your life, not expensive for your wallet. They are meant to help you create the life you want and the *you* that you want to be by creating a place full of beauty, space, and things that make you feel calm and peaceful.

A place you can truly call *home*.

BUT FIRST...

Before we get into any of that, let me offer one simple tip that you can do right now, one that can go a long, long way toward shifting the heavy, stuck energy of your home. One that, if you do not do one other thing, can still make your home feel so much lighter.

Clean. That's it - clean.

Cleaning absolutely changes the energy of a place immediately.

The top three things that give you the biggest bang for your cleaning buck are:

- Vacuum and sweep the floors.
- Take out the trash.
- Clean mirrors and windows. Bonus: once they're clean, they reflect/ let in more light, nature's natural energizer.

If you do just these three things, the energy within your house will begin to shift and it will immediately feel better to be in. Even better - you might be inspired to keep going, moving on to scrubbing the kitchen and baths. Before you know it, the whole place will feel significantly fresher.

Trust me, the girl who once hated cleaning so much she hid the dishes!

SO...

Read on for inspiration, tips, and tricks. Don't make the mistake of thinking things are too far gone for anything to make a difference. I assure you, even the smallest tweaks do. Have fun with it! Take the opportunity to flex some creative muscles. Don't let any voices of fear stop you (you know the ones - It's too hard, It'll take too long, I don't want to make a wrong decision, etc.).

There are no "wrong" answers, just chances to find what works for you and your home. This is absolutely not about perfection.

The ideas in this book are ones anybody can pull off without breaking the bank.

And if you think you don't have the time to do this, I absolutely promise this will end up giving you more time. When you curate your home and set yourself up for ease in your everyday life, you spend less time looking for things, tripping over things, reaching across things to get to other things...things like that.

2.

FEELING MORE AT HOME

"There is a magic in that little word, home; it is a mystic circle that surrounds comforts and virtues never known beyond its hallowed limits."

Robert Southey (English Romantic Poet)

Most of us live better than the kings of yore – especially when you factor in plumbing, running water, and electricity. And houses way back when (say, the 1500s and 1600s) were much smaller and more spartan than we are used to, often with only one to three rooms and only a few chairs, used on a rotating basis for meals and the like. I remember visiting Anne Hathaway's house (the wife of William Shakespeare, not the actress) in Stratford-upon-Avon, England. The house was so small I was struck when the guide explained that good old Bill courted Anne there, courting including getting her "in the family way" and requiring a quickie wedding to avoid scandal. *"How exactly did they manage that in this place?"* I wondered.

Maybe some of the courting happened elsewhere?

Whatever the layout or size of your home, why get caught up in conventions? If you've got the space, go ahead and turn that extra bedroom into a walk-in closet. And if you don't have much space, turn a corner of your bedroom into your office.

All that matters is what works for you so that your home feels like...you're home.

In my patio...a street sign from Zaragoza, Spain.

WHAT'S IN A WORD?

The Spanish word Querencia is a metaphysical concept that comes from the word "querer" or "to desire." Wikipedia defines it as "..the place where people feel most secure, gain the strength of their character and feel at home." Others add that it is the place where we are our most authentic selves.

In other words, querencia is the home we create for ourselves. So, what is your personal querencia? What does the word *home* mean to you? And how can you create that in your day-to-day life?

As I get older and shed some of the excesses from my life, I see that my inner querencia is much less elusive than it once was. (Donna Cameron / ayearoflivingkindly.com)

As I, myself, have gotten older, the word and the concept of home have come to mean so much to me, so much more than they ever had before. Where once I was gone all day (sometimes until midnight), now I'm working from home. The change has dramatically shifted both my priorities and my perspective.

What I've come to understand is this:

- Home is what we remember.
- Home is what we create for others to remember.
- Home is a place we miss when we're not there.
- Home is who we love.
- Home is who we are.

No matter where we've been – out to dinner with friends, to the most amazing concert ever, even on vacation to a tropical paradise – somehow it always ends with, "I want to go home." There truly is no place like it.

It's a place we rush back to so we can spend time with loved ones, indulge in some alone time, revel in the chance to let our hair down, and shake off the world.

The most touching text I have ever received was from my dear friend Teresa, commenting on some Christmas gifts she'd sent me. She said, "The reason why I decided on these gifts (for the home) actually is because your home reminds me of safety, warmth, and a loving place for me personally."

Not only is that text exceptionally moving, but it reminds me of how grateful I am to have a house that I can share with others.

A SAFE PLACE

I realize that many people are without a place to call home. According to the National Alliance to End Homelessness, every night nearly 600,000 people in the United States experience homelessness. Others who have a house don't feel safe there. All of which is heartbreaking, because everyone needs and deserves a home, and everyone needs and deserves to feel safe there.

For those of us fortunate enough to have a place to call home, and to feel safe there, we are all homemakers, whether we own or rent and whether we live alone, with roommates, a partner, multi-generations of adults (becoming more and more common), or five kids and counting.

My personal definition of a homemaker is someone who creates spaces in a house. We are all learning and trying.

Ultimately, the path of creating a home is a journey of and into the self. Let's get started on that path.

"I hope that you are coming home to yourself first, above all."

Ashley Beckman
(Dr. of Acupuncture and Chinese Medicine / drashley.com)

3.

BEAUTY IS EASIER THAN YOU THINK

"Everything is beauty, but not everyone sees it."

Confucius (Chinese Philosopher and Politician)

In nearly every discussion I have with friends these days, at some point the conversation turns to the concept of beauty, whether in nature, art, architecture, fashion, sports, you name it. I love this because as someone who grew up in Hollywood around the film industry, for most of my life I believed beauty was limited to the physical. I saw it as something granted from the heavens to a select group of humans deemed worthy or who had won the genetic lottery. But physical perfection is not what I'm hearing people talk about these days. What I'm hearing is a much broader definition than the media (traditional and social) try to sell us with all the retouched and perfectly filtered photos. Instead, I'm hearing appreciation for and exultation of things like a favorite coffee mug, the tree on the bluff overlooking the ocean, or new wallpaper.

Indeed, in its definition of beauty, Merriam-Webster includes the following:

> Beau*ty ~ noun, the quality or aggregate of qualities
> in a person or thing that gives pleasure to the senses or
> pleasurably exalts the mind or spirit.

By that definition, beauty is anything that positively affects us or anything we choose to call beautiful. By that definition, we all participate in and contribute to the beauty in this world, whether we're conscious of it or not. In other words, beauty is not found only in pretty faces or the celebrity mansions featured in *Architectural Digest*. It is in a sunset, in a laugh, in a kiss. And a beautiful life can be found in our surroundings. It is in a collection of teacups, a vintage photo in an art deco frame, a throw cushion on a couch. It is in whatever speaks to you, personally, as beauty.

What do you find beautiful? Take a minute now to make a list, but don't overthink it, just jot down what comes to mind. If you need a little inspiration, try thinking in categories – favorite animal, favorite color, favorite season (you might find Pinterest a great source of inspiration).

Here's my list:

- Kittens
- Sunsets on the beach
- Italian churches
- Peach-colored roses
- French Press and mug – ready to go for morning coffee
- Display of books
- Made bed

You may surprise yourself with an easy way to instantly add beauty to your surroundings. I hadn't thought of peach roses in years – and it was so easy to find a small inexpensive bunch at the supermarket! (The trick to buying roses at the market? Look for tighter buds – then cut stems and pluck off any fading outside petals before arranging in a vase.) You can brighten up your mornings with a welcoming bouquet in the bathroom, or distribute the blooms in small bud vases around the house to get the maximum bang for your buck.

A rose by any other color...

Whatever is on your list, it can contribute to making your home, and by extension your daily life, both beautiful and easy. Because, when it comes to our homes, beauty and ease are found in the intentional choice, use, organization, and display of the things we own. And there is nothing more beautiful or elegant than that kind of simplicity.

I'm not alone in this kind of thinking. Marie Kondo talks about things "sparking joy." The ancient Chinese art of feng shui is rooted in the energy of all things and how that energy affects us.

Consider a quote I read in *Realscreen* magazine (a publication devoted to reality and documentary TV and film). Years ago, Nancy Glass' company, Glass Entertainment Group, was having a tough go selling its first series, *Tanked*.

> "It was hard to sell," she recalls. "Everybody said: 'It's about fish tanks. People don't care about fish.' Of course they don't care about fish. They care about beauty."

Beauty speaks to us all. There's a reason museums exist, that we flock to Milan to see the Duomo, and that we literally stop and smell roses (peach or any other color).

In fact, if there's one thing I believe, it's that people want two things in their life, whether they can consciously articulate them or not. The first is ease. I mean, obviously, no one ever tries to take the harder road. Also known as flow or simplicity, ease makes our daily lives easier, which in turn makes our daily lives more joyful and less stressful. We know we have ease when we seem to move or transition effortlessly from one thing to another, when we can easily find what we are looking for without tripping over a million other things, when things just seem to flow. And things just seem to flow when our things are organized.

The other is beauty.

Beauty helps heal our traumas. Beauty feeds our souls and connects us to the Divine. And nowhere is beauty more powerful than in the home, the one place we know we can control, and the one where we spend so much of our time.

In fact, the reason I am writing this book is that I *so* believe that beauty in the home is crucial that I'm wanting to share it. To quote 13th-century poet Rumi, "Let the beauty we love be what we do."

Here's the thing, beauty is not something available only to a privileged few or only for special occasions. And ease is not something we experience only because the stars aligned or the gods were smiling down on us on a given day. Beauty and ease should be – and most certainly can be – available to all of us as our everyday experience in and of our homes. It just takes a little intentional investment of time and energy that will pay you back over and over in the future in your daily life.

To me, beauty in the home comes down to two things: curation and simplicity.

Cu*ra*tion ~ noun, the selection and care of objects to be shown in a museum or...an exhibit.
(per dictionary.cambridge.org)

Sim*pli*ci*ty ~ noun, freedom from difficulty or hardship. (per vocabulary.com)

To me, curation means living *only* with things you use, appreciate, and find valuable – monetarily or sentimentally. When I talk about simplicity, I mean things are set up so that they are easy to access and so that they support you in your daily life.

Curation plus simplicity creates elegance and beauty. In fact, Wikipedia defines elegance as "beauty that shows unusual effectiveness and simplicity."

Beauty is a life lived authentically.

Beauty is not special occasion. It is everyday and everywhere in our homes – in a pantry laid out just so, in the table fountain your cat drinks out of, in what you choose to hang on your wall, and in the candle on a table. In other words, beauty is in how we set up our homes so we can move through our days with more simplicity, allowing us to focus on the things that really matter – how we spend our time, with whom, and how we make them feel.

The Italians understand the importance of beauty in every area of life. They know its additive value. Think of the music, the wine, and the cafés where friends meet up on the daily. And they reflect it in their homes – in the eclectic pieces they cherish and place just so in the perfect spot and, of course, in the food they spend all day preparing with love for the traditional Sunday supper.

That kind of beauty is available to all of us, whether we own a 7,000 sq. foot mansion in Seattle or rent a studio walkup in Manhattan. And it doesn't have to break the bank. What it does have to do is be…

INTENTIONAL, FUNCTIONAL, AND INVITING – ESPECIALLY TO YOU.

INTENTIONAL

Anything done with intention affects the physical space. The smallest things can make a big impact.

So really consider what you want for, and from, your home. Do you want it to be a center for entertaining friends and family? Your own oasis from a crazy world? A space where your kids can run around, invite their friends over, and basically be kids? Or are you looking to update things now that the kids are out of the house? Have you gone through a divorce and want to start over with a place that represents your new life?

Take a few minutes and list the things you value that can be supported or reflected in your home environment. Start by free-flow writing. Once you've gotten everything down on paper, circle the top 5-10 things that you want to project with your home.

Some examples of these things and how they might be reflected in your home are:

- Travel – anything you brought back from places you've visited, such as photos, pencils, rugs, mugs, paintings - literally anything
- Adventure – a framed SCUBA certification, a photo of you jumping off a cliff into the sea
- Family – photos of your loved ones, artwork your kids did in school
- Reading – books on the shelf
- Sports – footballs, volleyballs, weights, bicycles, skis (displayed or put away as you see fit – no pun intended)
- Food – placemats, paper napkins with funny sayings on them, hanging pots and pans
- Music – a guitar left on a stand in the living room, a framed poster or ticket from the concert of your favorite band
- Fun – games, toys, etc.

Take some time to really get clear on these things, keeping in mind that you are not measuring yourself against anyone else – not the neighbor down the street nor the celebrity whose home was just featured in *House Beautiful*. Also take time to consider what season of life you are in. Lives change and evolve, and with them, needs. Have you just moved into your first place after graduating from college? Are you just starting a family or do you have kids in high school? Maybe you've recently decided to downsize. All these things will affect what you want in, and from, your home. They affect how you will set it up, allowing into it only those things that mirror you and your current priorities. This is about finding out what really matters to you now, not last year or last season.

FUNCTIONAL

Does your house simply work? Can you find things when you need them? Does everything have a place? Does everyone know where that place is? And does everyone have their own space when needed?

Are you actually using the things you have? So many people save things for that "special occasion," only pulling out the good china for the once-every-five-years formal dinner party. I had family members who never used the living room because the furniture was covered in plastic, to be taken off only when company came over. It never was. To me, that is the exact opposite of functional. Our things – even, especially, the nicest ones – are meant to be used, enjoyed, and appreciated. Otherwise, we are doing nothing but storing them.

Go ahead and use your best things all the time. Don't save them for some special event that may or may not happen. Think about it – how will we actually feel elegant and live elegantly if we never use our nicest things? Not using them shows that we're living in a mindset of lack.

My mother, who definitely had a mindset of lack and scarcity, was given a beautiful bed jacket that she kept in a box with special tissue paper. Having never deemed an occasion worthy of wearing it, one day she opened the box to find it had been eaten to bits by moths and was now also way too small. So, pull out that silver, pour a tall one into the crystal goblet, and don that dress because you can. Not using these things shows a lack of honoring, respecting, and appreciating them. And that is not the type of energy that will bring in more nice things.

Another thought about functionality: The concept of activation energy states that, basically, you are more likely to do something if that something takes no time to "activate." You are more likely to engage in cooking if the kitchen is clean (as opposed to having to clean it up first), to practice the piano if the sheet music is already out (or at least stored in the bench), to do needlepoint if your supplies are set up, right there next to a comfy chair and good lamp. In other words – shock of all shocks – we tend to do things when they are easy to do.

INVITING

Is your home a place people feel relaxed and welcome? More importantly, is it a place *you* feel relaxed and welcome? Because our homes make an impression – even on us, every time we come home. So, what is that impression? Does your place feel dark? Cold? Claustrophobic? Warm? Sunny? Lived in (in a good way)? Most importantly, does it feel loved, well-treated, and respected?

As you make your home more welcoming, as you become prouder of the space you have created, you might feel like inviting people over more, including those neighbors down the street. And this can be a very good thing. Studies have shown that socializing and maintaining relationships isn't only fun but can add years to your life. Connection and belonging are, after all, two of the hallmarks of Blue Zones®, communities across the globe where people live the longest.

CURATE YOUR HOUSE LIKE A MUSEUM. LIVE IN IT LIKE A HOME.

Sometimes curation means to add. Sometimes curation means to subtract. As stated above, it always means being intentional, functional, and inviting with what we choose to welcome into our homes.

Museums, as you know, curate collections and exhibitions, changing what's on view regularly. While I'm not suggesting you redecorate your home or change what's on display every six months (although you could!), I do advocate for the concept of easy in, easy out of the items in your house. As noted, we all have our seasons of life when certain things serve us, and those seasons and things change. There is no need to hold on to anything you no longer use, appreciate, or find value in, or which no longer makes you happy. There is something both freeing and uplifting about culling our possessions and just plain living with less stuff.

I certainly am not advocating for turning your home into a museum in terms of trying to achieve a level of perfection that is not only close to impossible, and certainly unsustainable, but actually makes it unlivable. If it is too perfect, nothing feels cozy, comfortable, or inviting. I have been in many a house that felt more like an exhibit than a home. I could not relax and get comfortable because everything felt so perfect I was scared to put anything out of its place. I was scared I would spill a drink (I have – more than once) and ruin the carpet, the chair, someone's outfit, a book on the table...you get the idea!

Life is real. Life gets messy – literally. This is not about perfection. The Japanese even have a term for the beauty of imperfection, *wabi-sabi*. So rather than trying to obtain some unobtainable level of perfection, think about setting up your home to reflect, support, and please you on a daily basis, through all your seasons as they change.

"Let us live for the beauty of our own reality."

Charles Lamb (English Essayist, Poet, and Antiquarian)

4.

IS YOUR HOME TELLING THE RIGHT STORY?

"If you're not the star of your own life, you're an extra in someone else's. Let your home be your perfect backdrop."

Cristina Gavin (Writer)

CBS News used to run a segment by Steve Hartman called *Everybody Has a Story*. He would fly to a randomly selected location in the U.S. (I think he used a dart thrown at a map.) Upon arrival, he'd randomly select a name from the town's old-fashioned phonebook. The lucky individual was the subject of that week's segment.

All of which is to say that you have a story and it is unique to you.

So what makes up your story? Things like:

- Your heritage
- Places you have lived and traveled
- Your favorite food
- Your hobbies
- Your career
- The people you love

These all capture our attention and say something meaningful because they let us know who you are and what you, yourself, find meaningful.

What's more, the things in our home that tell our story – where we come from, where we've been, and even where we hope to go – make us feel safe and comfortable, warm and embraced, because they represent us and the space we have created for ourselves in the world. One of the biggest mistakes you can make is to be too afraid to risk putting your real self and tastes on display. Perhaps these things were quashed out of you as a kid and you no longer even know what you like. I invite you to look inside and try to figure it out.

Get a pen and paper and simply journal for a few minutes. Write out:

- Where you come from
- Who you love
- What you enjoy
- Your favorite memories
- Places you've traveled
- Your accomplishments
- Your best traits
- Your favorite colors, tastes, sounds
- What you'd like others to know about you

FOR INSTANCE…

Here are some examples of things from my own life that help tell my story:

CHILDHOOD

As a child, my favorite toy was a wooden donkey with wheels which I pulled around on a rope. A few years ago I found it stuffed in a closet. I grabbed it and it now sits on a bookshelf in the living room. This was definitely out of my comfort zone. While I'd loved it too much to give away, until that point I hadn't made enough peace with my childhood to display memories of it.

Pulling my favorite toy as a child. I have no idea why I look so suspicious.

SOUVENIR

Walking down a street in Marrakech, I saw a wooden window for sale on the sidewalk, along with other arty knickknacks. It struck me as incredibly beautiful. I was sure I couldn't afford it. The fellow hawking the wares saw how lovely I thought it was. He also saw I was trying to leave. He kept calling me back and lowering the price every time I attempted an exit. Finally, he got down to $40 (US). No way I could walk away from that. I managed to lug it back to the States and it now hangs in my living room.

Bought this from a street vendor in Marrakech.

SOMETHING OLD

My mother was once at an auction and saw a nearly life-size wooden rocking horse. She planned to strip and repaint it, but when she stripped off the old paint, she realized it was much more charming with its worn patina. It sits still bare and unvarnished (so to speak) in the living room. Sometimes I even ride it.

Totally rideable.

CREDENTIALS & ARTWORK

My home office is decorated with certificates, a caricature of me, and two pieces of art by yours truly (such as they are, as I am no artist). It definitely reflects me and my experiences.

HOPES

I also have a vision board in my office. It is filled with things like photos of places I want to visit (hello, Tuscany and Bali), sayings and words I love ("flowy," "abundance"), and images of career hopes and dreams (feel free to tell Stanley Tucci I have a project for him!).

PHOTOS

I love photos of family and friends and have them all over the bookcase in the living room. Some of my favorites include one of my sister Maureen sitting on the beach laughing, my friend Becky's kids, and one of my friend Christina and me somewhere between Cancún and Chichen Itza, Mexico, exhausted from trying to navigate the roads in a rental car that kept breaking down.

NECESSITY

A French Press. My morning ritual includes a cup or two of freshly brewed coffee made in a metal cafetière. Nonnegotiable. And while visitors might not see this particular item, I love it and use it every day.

These things are all part of me and my story, of what matters to me. Some make me smile, others make me calm or inspire me. They all make me happy.

So, what things do you love? What tells your story? Your grandmother's wok? The pink shell your significant other found on the beach and gave to you? Perhaps the pieces of the board you chopped in half using your bare hands during a weekend retreat?

USE IT OR LOSE IT

This is not about aspiration or trying, and failing, because it is not actually possible, to reach some level of perfection as seen on Pinterest. This is about creating your real-life home.

Problem is, if you're keeping anything for any reason other than you really want it, you're either telling someone else's story or highlighting an unfortunate moment in your own.

SOMEONE ELSE'S STORY

Hiring an interior designer, keeping inherited pieces, and scouring websites for inspiration may seem like good ideas, but you run the risk of your home reflecting someone else rather than you and the ones you live with.

First and foremost, make sure your space is telling the story you want to tell.

AN UNFORTUNATE MOMENT

My mother had great taste and spent years working as an interior designer. Before turning pro, she hired a decorator to help do the family room. Good ole "Bob" (let's call him) came over one day to show her swatches for the couches. She'd just gotten home from foot surgery and was on who-knows-what painkillers. Bottom line, she agreed to two of his swatches. One a hideous pink plaid, the other an equally hideous purple plaid. Those couches stayed covered that way for eight years!

SHARED STORIES

Of course, this isn't necessarily about your story alone. If you live with roommates, a partner, kids, or other family members, your home should reflect all of you – as individuals and as a group.

And there's the rub. Because, beyond differences in color preferences or furniture layout, now we're getting into some very personal, often emotional, sometimes subconscious territory.

Designer and author Ingrid Fetell Lee put it this way in her blog, Aesthetics of Joy:

> ...*our space and our stuff are avatars for much deeper, more personal feelings about who we are and what we want out of life. To create a harmonious home, we need to get below the surface and start talking about how our individual desires relate to the shared idea of home that we're creating together.*
>
> ....*To resolve the tensions we have about style, ironically, we have to stop talking about the stuff, and start talking about our stories*

31

Think about designing a life, not decorating a home...
How do you want to live? What kind of life are you
building together, and how does your home help shape
that life?

Alone or in our personal tribe, we continue to evolve, individually and collectively. Our stories do, too.

"Everything to which we emotionally connect in our
homes has a story. Celebrating our stories is what
makes spaces feel like home."

Lawrence Biscontini, M.A.

(Mindful Movement Coach and Author / @findlawrence)

5.

THE SINGLE MOST IMPORTANT STEP FOR CREATING SIMPLICITY AND ELEGANCE

"The stuff you own has to help you create a life you want. And if it doesn't, why is it in your home?"

Peter Walsh (Author and Professional Organizer / peterwalshdesign.com)

The first law of creating an elegant, simple life is…say it with me:

Clear. The. Clutter.

I assure you, nearly every book, article, or blog ever written on improving your life, home, relationships, finances, or business starts with that basic principle. Clutter even affects your health. It is stuck energy and stuck energy is bad for the body and soul.

That said, I am a big fan of things. I love my stuff. I am in no way a minimalist. Too prescriptive, too restrictive for this gal. I aim to live a rich, abundant life. So, when I talk about getting rid of clutter, I'm not talking about downsizing nor suggesting you chuck it all and move into an RV, unless that is what calls you. If it is, go for it and I'll be sure to follow you on social.

Clearing clutter is free and the fastest way to create a more elegant home and a simpler life.

The truth is most of us have more than enough stuff and overconsuming is neither necessary nor healthy for our psyches or our wallets. As for the planet, there's an environmental cost to producing, transporting, and disposing of goods.

What I am advocating is intentionality with what we purchase and what we allow into our homes. If we allow stuff in indiscriminately, we are not setting standards about what we accept into our lives. And what kind of message does that send the Universe?

That said, if you're feeling overwhelmed by the amount of stuff that has taken up residence in your residence, you are not alone. A survey by Decluttr (spelled like that) and the National Association of Professional Organizers revealed that 54% of Americans are overwhelmed by clutter and 78% have no idea what to do with it.

STUCKNESS

Clut*ter ~ transitive verb, to fill or cover with scattered or disorganized things that impede movement or reduce effectiveness. (per merriam-webster.com)

If you're feeling stuck in any area of your life, chances are there's some clutter in the way. Clutter isn't just the physical papers, stuffed closets, and disorganized garages...*it's also the energy attached to all that stuff.*

When these objects are cleared, life opens up in ways that can feel like magic. New opportunities, romance, and improved health are just some of the things that can come our way. When we throw out stuff we don't use, appreciate, or find value in, we invite in the chance to break through blocks that have been holding us back for years, whether we've been aware of them or not.

I consider my home a sacred place, which means I aim to treat it as such (even if my cats have their own definition of how things should be treated). Honoring your home environment shows you value it and yourself. Clutter, on the other hand, shows a lack of respect for ourselves, the people we live with, and our homes.

WHAT IS CLUTTER? WHY DOES IT HAPPEN?

Not all mess is clutter. Some messes are things that have a home and just need to be put away. Things like that stack of dishes in the sink or the pile of laundry on the bed. But all clutter creates a mess.

Just as often as being piled up everywhere, clutter is stuff that has been relegated to some place like the back of a closet, the attic, the garage, or anywhere we neither see it nor use it. In my home, I have found that clutter is anything I "trip" over trying to get to something else. Clutter is things that no longer add value to your life (if they ever did) and things that stand between you and the life you want to live. Things become clutter as you change, as your life changes.

Clutter is best dealt with by a good session of personal introspection before anything else. Ask yourself why you are holding on to certain items.

Get out a pen and paper. Set a timer for ten minutes. Write about the clutter, mess, or things in your life, and why you've been holding on to them. Don't check yourself, just put down whatever pops into your mind. Keep writing for the entire ten minutes without letting your hand leave the page.

To get you started, here are some reasons we hold on to things we no longer need or love, if we ever did:

- **Something's Missing**: Often we fill spaces in order to fill something within ourselves. In other words, we are compensating because we feel incomplete or as though something is missing.
- **Guilt**: It was a gift from Aunt Sally, your college roommate, the woman at the vet's office. Gifts are lovely and to be appreciated. Say "Thank you" graciously and think of who else might enjoy or get use out of that desk coffee warmer that you'll never take out of the box.
- **Inherited**: You inherited it and, what the heck, it was free. I have many inherited items and I love them, but the truth is, after too many you run the risk of your place not seeming like "You."
- **Sentimental Journey**: It belonged to your mom, dad, uncle, long-lost cousin once removed, and even if you don't really like it, you can't bring yourself to give it away or toss it. It's not really your taste and you have no place for it, so it sits in a closet collecting dust. My sister recently showed me a quilt our great-aunt had made. Did I want it? No, thank you, not really me. But it was cool to know the story behind it. Goes to show you can love the story but not the thing.
- **Fixable**: You're holding on to something that is broken, no longer working, or missing a part or piece (like a puzzle) in the hopes you'll find someone to repair it, the item will magically come back to life, or the piece will somehow show up.

- **Storage Unit**: Your house has become a storage unit for your adult children or any other family member or friend. No. Just no. If they don't live there, why does their stuff? Anything they want stays with them. Your home is for living, not storing.

- **Someday**: You never know when you, or someone you know, once knew, or might meet may need or want it. Never mind that you've never used it, despite allowing it to reside in your house for the past however many years.

- **Kids**: Your children may want it someday. Maybe. Then again, maybe not. They may not share your taste and appreciation for certain items. Ask them. Let them know you're going through things and to "Speak now or forever hold your peace."

- **Wishful Thinking**: Somehow, miraculously, this house will gain more storage space for all of the things I'm not currently willing to deal with.

- **Cost**: You spent money on it. Sorry, but that money is not coming back by you keeping it. If the item is in good condition, you might be able to make a little something by selling it online or at a consignment store.

- **Trust**: You don't trust your own taste and are afraid of making a wrong decision.

- **Fear #1**: You are scared to give things away because you are scared of the future. What if something happens and I don't have anything else?

- **Fear #2**: You are scared to be seen – and perhaps judged – for what you do keep and display. Clutter offers you the excuse of things "being in transition" or "a work in progress."

As you can see, clutter is procrastination – a bunch of delayed decisions. I was tempted to write "indecision" rather than "delayed decisions," but when we put off dealing with clutter (or anything else, for that matter), we have made the decision not to decide...for now. The problem is that putting off those decisions keeps us stuck.

First recognized in thermodynamics, the law of entropy states that as a system loses more and more energy (as it inevitably will), it disintegrates into chaos. Which basically means don't worry, if you don't do anything about it, it will get worse. So, at some point, something's got to give. But why live that way? It takes effort to turn a habit around, but it's worth it.

First step – you have to get past the excuses that are keeping you stuck. Excuses like:

- I'm too busy.
- My kids will just make a mess again.
- I'll shove it in the garage and get to it eventually. No one sees what's in there.
- What if I need this someday?

What these voices are really trying to do is protect the status quo, to keep you from taking a look at the reasons you've been holding on to things. Looking means taking a look at yourself and your motivations, as well as your level of willingness to commit to unsticking your life.

When you can't let go of something, it won't let go of you. In other words, if you are not willing to take an honest look at the clutter, you are just allowing it to hold you hostage.

THE SIDE EFFECTS OF CLUTTER

Clutter sucks and drains the energy out of almost every area of our lives. To wit:

- Time
- Vitality and energy
- Productivity
- Creativity
- Ability to focus
- Relationships (lack of intimacy of all kinds, poor communication, discord, flared tempers)
- Career
- Money
- Ability to move beyond old patterns
- Social interactions (these may either be avoided or full of drama)
- Activity level/exercise
- Life satisfaction

Clutter negatively affects these areas because it is literal stuff, stuck energy, between you and them. More tangibly, clutter has been linked to:

- Unwanted weight
- Sleep issues
- Depression
- Anxiety
- Memory issues
- Increased levels of cortisol (living in clutter is stressful, and stress is not just a buzz kill, it's a killer)

Not to mention the potential for tripping (literally) and, in severe cases, increased toxic mold and fire hazards.

CLUTTER AND LONELINESS

Clutter can also be isolating because if your place is a mess you may tend not to invite people over. Or you may lack the energy to go out. Furthermore, the space taken up by clutter is very effective at making sure there's no room for anyone or anything else to enter.

Clutter literally cuts you off from new people, things, and opportunities.

WHAT HAPPENS WHEN YOU DECLUTTER

The first thing that happens when you declutter is that you turn your house into more of a home. The second is that your home becomes more user-friendly. Your sense of calm and wellbeing will almost certainly increase.

That's because you'll have created space for those new people, things, and opportunities to come in – space for more abundance, better relationships, and improved health and weight. (Getting rid of things is literally taking weight off and can, in fact, lead to weight loss, if that is your goal.) It's like the quote (attributed to many different people), "In order to pick something up, you first have to put something down." In order to be able to receive, we need to first release and create space.

Here's the exciting part: As you curate and get rid of things, deciding what you no longer want and what no longer serves you, you create this amazing opportunity to decide what you *do* want and what *will* serve you. You get to declare how you want your life to look, what you would like it to reflect, and who you want to be within it.

Clearing clutter helps you live with intention, in alignment with, and clarity around, what you say your priorities are.

Priorities like family, music/playing an instrument, volunteering, reading, learning a new language – the list is endless. You are literally freeing up time to devote to these things because you are no longer spending so much time cleaning, maintaining, putting away, and otherwise dealing with and being drained by a bunch of stuff.

HOW TO DECLUTTER

"Declutter" sounds negative, so let's start by clearing that up.

We are not deciding what to get rid of. We are deciding what to keep – what we truly choose to have in our lives.

There are no rules around this, just the opportunity to feel into what would feel good for you. I believe life is expansive. We are ever-growing and evolving, so this is not about restricting, rather, it is about inviting expansion and evolution to take place.

The next step is to set the stage. The process of decluttering can be emotional as we get transported back to a different time in our lives. You may come up against regret, self-judgment, nostalgia, and even loss.

Clearing clutter can hit buttons. If you grew up without a lot of things or have emotional baggage around money and lack, the thought of getting rid of stuff can really bring up…stuff. Recognize and thank whatever is coming up, see what's behind it, and continue when it feels appropriate. It's OK to take a pause, for however long, to make sure you are focused and calm.

PRIORITIES

Decluttering starts with a vision of what you want from and in your home, as well as what you want from and in your life.

I know our values should be obvious to us, and for the most part they are, but a little sleuthing in the form of a tried-and-true exercise can be very illuminating.

Ready?

Write down as many values as you hold/can think of – try getting to fifty or even a hundred. Things like:

- Honesty
- Family
- Travel
- Generosity
- Nurturing
- Volunteering
- Education
- Wisdom
- Etc.

Whittle the list down to twenty.

Now take it down to fifteen.

Now take it down to ten.

(Sidenote: I've taken it down even further and end up with kindness, integrity, and spirituality as my top three.)

What you're left with are your top values, which reflect the kinds of things you should have and keep in your home. For instance, wisdom can be reflected in books. Education could be a framed diploma. Nurturing might be found in the loaf pan you bake banana bread in for friends.

ASSESS THE SITUATION

So many of us get so used to our clutter that we fail to see it. So, take a tour and investigate your own home. Walk around with fresh eyes, assessing how it looks and how it makes you feel. If you'd like, make a list of "to-dos."

Once you've got a realistic take on what's going on in your home, ask yourself some clarifying questions. Again, journaling really helps here and you may be surprised what you end up writing. Don't worry, this is only for you – no one else has to see it.

- *Why* do I want to declutter? (To make my space more beautiful? To make my life simpler? To create a sense of calm in my home?)
- Why do I own this?
- How did I come to own this? Did someone give it to me? Do I have any emotions (positive or negative) around that story or person?
- Do I love this item?
- Do I use it?
- Do I need it?
- Do I find it beautiful?
- Does it bring me happiness?
- Will it support me in creating ease and simplicity in my life?
- What benefit does it bring to my life? (Joy and beauty absolutely count, as does utility.)
- Does it represent me now? (Not the me of last year or five years ago.)
- Does it fit into my home?
- Does it fit into my life?

- Does it fit with how I want my home and life to function? To look?
- Am I trying to fix or prove anything by owning so much stuff? Am I attempting to fill a void within me? That is not a job any one thing, or any collection of things, can do. That is a job you are going to have to take on yourself.
- Is this something my family will want someday? The concept of Swedish Death Cleaning (yep, that's a thing, called *döstädning* in Swedish) asks what your family would have to go through (literally, not emotionally) if something happened to you. Take a look at what you own. Tell your family the stories behind the items. Discuss what's valuable, what they might want, and feel free to get rid of anything else. Your loved ones will have less work to do should anything – God forbid – happen to you.

If the things you own are not supportive of the life you desire to live, then it's time to let them go. Even things with sentimental value. The memories and love do not reside in the thing, they reside in our hearts and minds. Clearing the clutter creates the space which allows us to create new memories. If it doesn't add to your life, it doesn't belong in your life.

AVOIDING OVERWHELM

Depending on how much stuff there is and how long it's been there, clutter clearing can be *a lot*.

Start small – small victories count, big time.

Set a timer for just ten minutes. Pick one place that's easy to clear and get started. Maybe it's a game shelf. Or your makeup drawer. Just doing one shelf or drawer can powerfully shift energy and inspire you to keep going.

Make it fun. Put on some music and dance. Celebrate every victory. A bubble bath, a cuddle with your cat, or a walk outside are all free and great ways to acknowledge yourself for every step forward. Get the whole household involved and make it a game. Word on the street is kids actually love this. (Well, young kids, anyway – maybe not surly preteens and teens.)

Once you feel ready to dive in, start by going room by room, starting with the easiest sections of the easiest rooms. One at a time, empty every drawer, shelf, cabinet, and closet. Then scrub, dust, and clean it.

Next – start to cull.

This is where curation begins. Tap into what you love.
What things speak to you? Which do you use?
Which represent who you are now and who you want to
be moving forward?

For each drawer, shelf, cabinet, or closet, only put back what you have intentionally chosen to keep, making sure it fits both the physical space and your life. Put these items back with fresh eyes. Sometimes just a little thing like rolling rather than folding towels can make all the difference in making something look nice and organized – even elegant – in a way that is easy to maintain.

Decisions. Decisions. Decide what stays, not what goes.

You'll want four boxes or bins:

- Things that can be repurposed for use somewhere else in the house (maybe a flowerpot would make a great pen and pencil holder)
- Things to be donated (the sooner this bin gets out of the house, the better, otherwise it remains as clutter)
- Things you can sell (by consignment or online)
- Things to gift or pass on to a friend or family member

As you go through each room or area, the point is to find every item a place in your home or a home in someone else's place.

Anything to be thrown away gets tossed immediately. Be sure to keep an eye out for unnecessary duplicates (e.g., phone chargers) and anything you can easily find online (e.g., owner's manuals).

And it goes without saying you want to ditch anything that holds any negative memories or associations whatsoever – that t-shirt from your ex, the mug from the job that fired you. No matter how lovely, things do carry energy and we're only looking for good juju.

As mentioned earlier, this process can bring up a lot of emotions. You may need to forgive yourself for the mistakes of the stuff you have.

Why did I spend money on that?

Why have I been holding on to this?

Remember that you were doing the best you could at the time. The past does not matter. What matters is being true to yourself in the present. As the saying goes, "Let go of your past and your past will let go of you."

A caveat: Yes, it is possible to go overboard with getting rid of things. You don't want "Binner's Remorse." Never chuck something just because you think you "should" for whatever reason. If there's something you feel on the fence about, put it away for a while. By the time you pull it out again months later, you will have a clearer head about it.

It is important to be intentional every step of the way – from acquiring to releasing possessions.

HOW NOT TO DECLUTTER

Do not declutter by organizing.

*Organizing is not decluttering – it's merely
straightening the clutter up. Moving stuff around and/
or shoving it in drawers is not decluttering.*

And do not declutter by getting a storage unit. You will have to go through everything eventually. A storage unit just offers you the chance to pay someone else for the privilege of putting that off.

According to Carla Fried, writing for Rate.com:

There are an estimated 45,000 storage facilities across the country...an estimated 6.5 square feet of self-storage space for every person in America...Households, not companies, account for 80% of industry revenue of $38 billion a year...

The average monthly cost is about $1 per square foot, but in many urban areas it stretches to about $1.50 or more per square foot...(all told) that works out to nearly $2,000 a year to store stuff.

When you look at it that way, you start to realize it might be cheaper to replace most of the things you are storing than pay for a unit year after year.

*Chances are you don't have too little storage – you have
too much stuff.*

You don't need to sell your house and buy a bigger one. You also don't need to get rid of all your stuff and get a smaller house. You just need to make some intentional decisions, including whether paying for storage is easier than a commitment of time to, as they say, just do it.

Be gentle and stay present with yourself so you can hear the voice of intuition as you go through this process.

ORGANIZE, STORE, AND DISPLAY...WHEN THE TIME IS RIGHT

Once you've dealt with the clutter, then you can deal with the mess. In other words, that's the time to start thinking about organization and storage, maximizing the space you have for what you are keeping. Could you use some plastic shoe boxes? Shelf dividers? Hooks? Drawer organizers? Bins, baskets, canisters, and a good label maker are invaluable tools for creating an organizational system that is functional and sustainable.

For everything that isn't stored in a closet, cupboard, or drawer, you can really get creative and have fun with what you display – things like vignettes on shelves, tables, and walls.

Start asking yourself, "What do I want surrounding me? How do I want to feel? Inspired? Calm? Full of dreams of adventure?"

How can you make what you put out the most representative of you, what you care about, and what you desire? Whether it's a wall gallery of photos, a collection of teaspoons, anime, or magnifying glasses, make it the "youest" it can be.

You can also have fun making pieces – inherited items, vintage finds, gifts, even something which was mass-produced – your own. A change of hardware, new fabric, or a coat of paint can breathe new life into any number of items, allowing them to reflect your taste and personality.

That said, don't buy anything related to organization before you've finished decluttering. You won't really know what or how much you need and you may be able to repurpose things you already own.

So, don't think about the "what" and "where" of storage and display until you see what you actually end up with. You may surprise yourself by what you end up keeping and not keeping, and by what physical space has opened up.

HOW TO KEEP THE CLUTTER FROM COMING BACK

Of course, clutter clearing is not a "one and done." You never finish decluttering - because the bad news is that your life is constantly evolving. The good news is that your life is constantly evolving.

So, once you've shown the clutter the door, how do you keep it from walking back in?

Consider:

- Make intentional, wise purchases. (Bonus: Buying intentionally equals buying less, which equals spending less, which equals financial savings!)
- Choose the best quality you can afford. High-quality products last longer, leading to less waste and less need to replace things. As a wise person once said, "Buy the best. Cry once."
- Consider what you are looking for from the product. A treadmill might mean you want to exercise more. A new pan could symbolize entertaining friends. Can the same desire be met without having to purchase anything new?
- Remember that the more functional/diverse an item, the fewer things you will need to purchase.
- Follow the maxim (generally attributed to feng shui) of filling up no more than 80%, preferably 50%, of any visible space or surface (such as a shelf, counter, or table).
- When you're done using something, put it away rather than putting it down.

"INVISIBLE" CLUTTER

Clutter clearing isn't just limited to stuff. It's about decluttering your life on all levels, including:

- Your Time: Are there things you can just say no to? Are there things you can take off your calendar? What can you delegate?
- Your Mind: For me, taking walks is a great way to clear my head. Meditation is also a great way to connect to yourself.
- Your Heart: What helps you move past hurt, anger, and resentment? I love to call a friend and vent. You may want to beat a pillow.

Decluttering in these areas will, again, allow you to use your energy in ways that match your priorities.

Most importantly, set your own boundaries around how you treat your home and what and how much you will invite in to live there with you. Boundaries are beautiful things. Say no when you mean no. When you say yes and don't mean it – to people, plans, things – you become a liar, to yourself and to what you say you prioritize.

Ultimately, this is not just about setting up your home, it's about setting up your life and the way you show up and operate within that life.

Finally, one of the greatest rewards of clutter clearing is the confidence you will find to express yourself more fully and authentically – at home and out in the world. "Be yourself – everyone else is already taken."

"What I know for sure is that when you declutter – whether it's in your own home, your head, or your heart – it is astounding what will flow into that space that will enrich you, your life, and your family."

Peter Walsh
(Author and Professional Organizer / peterwalshdesign.com)

6.

PLEASING THE SENSES

"I go to nature to be soothed and healed, and to have my senses put in order."

John Burroughs (American Naturalist)

Our ancient forebears lived outdoors, in nature, finding shelter where they could. This meant they were constantly surrounded by natural sights, sounds, tactile experiences and textures, smells, and tastes. As if we couldn't have guessed, research has shown that when we modern folk create spaces for ourselves which reflect nature and are pleasing to all our senses, we tend both to feel better and to live better lives. Echoing nature just makes sense. There is nothing inauthentic in nature and there is much grace, simplicity, wisdom, and truth in how things work in the natural world. Enter biophilic design.

In a nutshell, biophilic design creates interiors that take into consideration the five senses. It aims to echo nature and make us feel good emotionally and physically, thus improving our overall well-being. Acknowledging the therapeutic power of design, biophilic-designed houses are meant to elicit positive sensory reactions from anyone who enters them. What's more, they take into account that we are sensual creatures relating to the world through sight, sound, touch, smell, and taste.

When designing our homes, we usually just think of how things will look to the eyes, ignoring the other senses. But we want our homes to speak to all of our senses, perhaps even including the sixth. After all, how each of our senses is stimulated affects us, making us stressed, happy, calm, anxious, etc.

Obviously, what we're wanting sensually from any one room will be dictated by the function of the space and the purpose we want it to serve. We want different things from our living rooms, bedrooms, kitchens, etc., and we want each to feel a certain way.

If we are the star of the movie of our lives, then we need the right set. Take a sensory inventory of your home. Walk into each room and decide how you want the "set" to look, sound, feel, and smell.

"Design is so important because chaos is so hard."
Jules Feiffer (Cartoonist and Author)

I SEE YOU

First impressions, or judgments, based on sight happen instantaneously. Literally. Within a split second of looking at something we've made up our minds whether we like it or not. Whatever room you walk into in your home, what is the first visual impression it gives? Formal? Cozy? Jarring due to too many bold patterns? Industrial?

Several elements work together to make up the look of a room.

COLOR

Color is energy – and particular colors cause us to have certain unconscious visceral (energetic) reactions. It is interesting to note how these reactions correlate to idioms in the English language. Consider both the associated feelings and sayings of a color when evaluating the impressions different areas of your home are giving. Then make tweaks to call in a sense of upliftment, relaxation, sophistication, play, or whatever it is you're going for.

Red is said to boost passions (both positive and negative), energy, and appetite. Orange is also associated with increased energy. Yellow is said to amp up both energy and metabolism, while at the same time being cheerful and inviting. Hence, when used together, red, orange, and yellow give us the Golden Arches and Kings of the burger world (as well as many other chains). In language, someone who is "in the red" may be spending money too energetically. Someone cheerful is described as having a "sunny" (yellow) personality.

In the home, red is best used in public areas like the entryway or living room. It also makes a great accent color for furniture or décor. In feng shui, red doors, especially where a street dead ends, are often considered auspicious (there are caveats depending on which "school" of feng shui you subscribe to). Orange is super-energizing so is best used in moderation and in a place where lots of activity happens, like a kid's playroom. Living rooms, kitchens, bathrooms, and dining rooms can all be made sunny and bright with a pop (or more) of yellow, as long as it's in a shade that doesn't amp up the energy too much.

On the other end of the spectrum, colors such as teal, lavender, and coral can be very calming and are often used in day spas. The rarely used phrase "laid out in lavender" means, in part, to show something in its best light. These colors, depending on their exact tones, can be used in bedrooms, bathrooms, and even offices. Darker purples can make a sophisticated statement in a living room.

Pink is associated with being frothy, calming, and carefree. In feng shui it is the color of love. If you are "in the pink," you are healthy and doing well. Personally, I think of pink as something best used sparingly, perhaps in a side table or pillow.

Green and brown are considered evocative of nature. When we "green" our homes we are making them more eco-friendly. Brown, being the color of earth, grounds us. Since there is so much to appreciate in and about nature, it stands to reason that we would want to incorporate these colors into our homes. Because there are so many tones and because they are considered so close to nature, these two can pretty much pull duty in any space, giving it a sense of both calm and warmth.

In general, blue is seen as neutral and traditional. Some say it weakens appetite. Others believe blue offices support productivity. Of course, there are many different shades of blue. Darker blue may be associated with being "blue," depressed and melancholy. Likewise, Blues music sings about being depressed and melancholy. So, a bit of moderation is called for when using the darker tones. Conversely, light blue may be uplifting and reflect the idea that "the sky's the limit." These lighter blues are especially great for bedrooms and bathrooms or as a pop of color on a ceiling.

Gray can be modern or classic. Intense or subtle. Many designers consider it incredibly versatile, claiming it works in almost any room. Others think it's a trend that has come and gone. The definition of "gray area" includes the idea of no clear rules. So go ahead and think out of the box and use it as you see fit, if you see fit.

Black doesn't even appear on the color wheel as it is the absorption of all colors. While it may be elegant in some circumstances (think black-tie clothing), it is also considered somber, sad, and cold. Employees of CBS in New York City derisively refer to the network headquarters building as "Black Rock" not just because of its look, but because that's where you're called when you are in trouble or about to be fired. Someone who is "black-hearted" has no feelings for others. "Black Monday" refers to the Stock Market crash of 1987, while "Black Tuesday" references the crash of 1929. And black can have a really negative impact on our emotions. When I first got to college, we were told that we were not allowed to paint our dorm rooms black. Not that I wanted to. But apparently, someone had the year before and ended up killing himself. While I can't place all the blame on the black room, I'm sure it didn't help. I invite you to use black sparingly.

White, of course, is incredibly popular and versatile in home design. Clean, bright, and even innocent, it can create a greater feeling of space and light. When you "whitewash" something, you're trying to clean it up, which in the home may be a very good thing. White works in any room. I particularly like it in kitchens and bathrooms. But, of course, don't overdo even this workhorse. When overused, it can seem cold, stark, industrial, or just plain lacking in imagination and daring. Colors that are just slightly off-white tend to have a bit more warmth to them.

Finally, while a new coat of paint can spruce up and freshen any room, a good paint job (unless you DIY it) can cost a whole lot of money. Remember that pops and accents of color here and there can make a big difference toward achieving the effect you want without the time and expense of a major redo.

That said, the most important thing to ensure is that your color choices reflect you and your personality. Own that and stay true to it. Color trends in home design come and go (think Pantone® Color Of The Year) and you need not participate in any of them if they don't speak to you. Keep in mind that the colors that look good on you in clothing are the same ones you should use in painting and decorating your home. After all, you will be seen in and next to these things.

"I won't even sit on an avocado-colored couch."
Ali McGraw (Actress)

It's no good if "this year's color" looks great in a magazine if it drains you of all life when you stand next to it. Your home has to look good *on* you. For me, I look horrible in and near anything gray.

LIGHTING

The next element to consider in designing the look of a room is light. Are there windows that let in sunlight during the day? What direction do they face? In the Northern Hemisphere, southern-facing rooms may need to have the sunlight tempered, perhaps adding sheer curtains as window treatments. North-facing rooms may need mirrors or special paint to allow in more light.

You want to find the perfect balance between too bright and too dark, which can change with the time of day. Lighting which is too dim has been shown to lead to anxiousness and lack of alertness. Lighting which is too bright can feel jarring and unsettling. In other words, lighting can calm you down or amp you up.

Lighting also affects our circadian rhythm, which regulates the sleep-wake cycle. Dim light signals that it's bedtime. Bright light keeps us awake. Dimmer switches offer the opportunity to adjust as time of day and situation require. Three-way lightbulbs can also do the trick. Beware of LEDs with too much blue light. Just like too much late-night screen time, they can really throw the body clock off.

Flat lighting can make things seem just that, flat and dull. Conversely, you can use lights to create a focal point in a room, such as a wall sconce or an art lamp on a painting. Floor lamps can also be used for accent lighting, while desk lamps help illuminate work areas. Layering light from different sources tends to work best to give a room that just-right illumination.

Lightbulbs can be warm or cool in tone, harsh or soft. Just ask anyone in the film business. Overhead lights free up space but can cast unflattering shadows. A lighting plan that incorporates strategically placed and pointed lamps can be kinder to faces and easier on the eyes.

Taken together, color and light can visually create and change the shape and size of a room and its furnishings. Lighter colors and more lighting create a greater sense of space. And while darker hues and moodier lighting may feel cocooning, they will also cause a room to seem smaller, which you may want if you're trying to keep things intimate.

IT'S ALL ABOUT THE SCALE

No, I'm not talking about the one in the bathroom (never!). I'm talking about the proportion of your furniture and décor in relation to the space it's in. To quote designer and author Ingrid Fetell Lee:

Scale...has a powerful impact on the way we feel in a space. When the furnishings in a room feel proportionate to the space and our bodies, it sets us at ease. When they're too big or too small, they make us feel awkward, like our bodies are too clunky for our space, or vulnerable — exposed and unprotected.

THE SHAPE OF THINGS

Now, let's talk about shapes. How does a straight-back chair make the room feel? What feeling does a curve on the back of a sofa evoke in you?

Curves, straight lines, and other geometric shapes all add visual interest and emotion to a room, especially when mixed together.

SAY WHAT?

Sounds mean more to a home than we may realize. Just ask anyone who has tried to sell a house close to a freeway. Personally, the sound of the fan on a stove makes me incredibly anxious and on edge. On a positive note, we can utilize sound in a number of different ways for a number of different, more pleasant purposes. In fact, many cultures and traditions have used sound and music as therapy for centuries to treat everything from depression to sleep disorders to blood pressure and even brain injuries. Like so many other modalities, this form of sensory therapy, which can include everything from music to sound baths to Binaural beats (specific tones played through stereo headsets), has suddenly become popular across the United States.

In the home, features like singing bowls, crackling fires, and windchimes can help create a calming and cozy atmosphere. Anything that makes you feel good will work. I *love* the sound of my tea kettle whistling – it sounds like a train leaving a station and makes me so happy. Music can be used to calm, take a dance break, set the mood for a party, or for…whatever.

All aboard!

A common stagnant energy "cure" in the tradition of feng shui is placing a tabletop fountain near the front door. The motion creates energy while the water gives off uplifting negative ions and sounds like a babbling brook.

FEELINGS

Touch may be the most sensual of all the senses. When you think about it, we are never not touching something. As I write this, I am touching a chair. I hardly ever wear shoes at home so if I go to the kitchen to get water, my bare feet will touch the hardwood floor.

In what way are you creating the "feel" of your home? A mixture or layering of materials and textures helps create the most elegant and sensual of environments. Plus, textures and materials that feel good never go out of style.

To get you thinking in the right direction, consider:

- Thick carpets feel luxurious.
- A velvet headboard in the bedroom can make you feel très sexy.
- Leather chairs can be comfy, while also giving off an air of formality and a commanding presence.
- Tile floors feel cool all year round.
- Throw blankets are super cozy and perfect for a night in front of the TV.

MEMORIES

The materials in our homes – wood, leather, cotton, wool – all have a smell. Everywhere we go, every place we step into (homes, restaurants, stores, offices) or out to (streets, mountains, parks) has a smell.

> Smell, the most long-lasting of all sense memories, can even trigger memories. Author Vladimir Nabokov said, "Nothing revives the past so completely as a smell that was once associated with it."

Seriously, hasn't a smell ever transported you right back to someplace else? For me, it's the smell of the soapy oil my grandmother used to put in her big tub when my sister and I would take a bath. I can buy a bottle of it any time to relive the moment. If yours is cookies baking in Mom's oven, consider whipping up a batch. If it's the scent you remember from camping, try some pine essential oil in a diffuser.

A diffuser keeps your home smelling, and feeling, fresh.

Scents create a mood, from cozy to luxurious. They can also affect our moods, making us relaxed or jittery, or putting us *"in the mood."* Step up your smell game at home by enlisting the help of candles, flowers, plants, diffusers, fruit in a bowl, room sprays, and the like. If you want to vary scents throughout the year, consider the seasons – warm, spicy, and woodsy for fall and winter; fresh, citrus, floral, and cool for spring and summer. Be aware, though, that many things containing "fragrance" are actually toxic. To keep exposure minimal, make sure that any scents you use in your home are 100% organic.

MMM...

The kitchen and dining room are not the only places where taste plays a factor in the home. While I love the concept of libraries, any place where I can't eat or drink (or talk, for that matter) is no place I want to hang out. All of this is to say, it's always nice to be within easy reach of food and drink. Things like having a coaster and table available for a cup of coffee or placing a bowl of fruit, chocolates, or nuts in your home office are easy ways to make this happen.

THE SIXTH SENSE

The final thing you want to zero in on for every space is how you feel when you're in it. Yes, I'm talking about the "vibe" of a room.

Whether or not you believe in a specific "sixth" sense, we respond to signals registered on an unconscious level, including the overall feeling in any given space. Even after you've put thought into enhancing all five senses in a room, you may feel something is just "off." Trust your intuition or gut reaction about how a space makes you feel, avoiding the temptation to override that *knowing* with logic.

TRY THIS EXERCISE

Go ahead and sit down in every area. Does the dining room need a boost of energy? Is the living room calling out for seating arranged in a way to foster more conversation, thus fostering more connection? Are you looking for an oasis of calm in a bathroom? Maybe you just want a sense of fun and whimsy throughout your entire home. What tweaks can you incorporate to make these things happen?

"Nothing can cure the soul but the senses, just as nothing can cure the senses but the soul."

Oscar Wilde (Irish Poet, Playwright, and Aesthete)

PART 2

SIMPLICITY AND ELEGANCE ONE ROOM AT A TIME (AND ON THE GO)

7.

ENTRYWAY – MAKING YOUR HOME WELCOMING

"A smile is the universal welcome."

Max Eastman (American Writer, Poet, and Activist)

Cliché has it you only get one chance to make a first impression. Not so fast. Truth is, your home makes an impression on you again and again and again, every time you step through your front door. And it's the same impression every single time – calm and inviting or chaotic and claustrophobic from too much stuff. That energy can either support you or weigh you down, starting the second you step foot inside.

And when it's somebody new walking through the door, the impression they get is not only of your home but of you. Chances are you already know, but take a step outside your front door and step back in with the intention of discerning what someone else might feel when walking in for the first time.

In feng shui the entry and front door represent where you receive abundance of health, wealth, relationships, etc. They also represent what you show to the world and how it sees you. My friend Amber is so acutely aware of the impression and vibe she wants her house to offer that she has named it the "Amber Inn." Her intention is for people to feel welcomed and cared for. I'm all about a Zen, Southern California feel.

Whatever vibe you're going for, when your home feels welcoming – to you or anyone else – it is also welcoming to new things, people, and opportunities.

Come on in.

PULLING DOUBLE DUTY

The conflict within the entryway is that it tends to serve two very different purposes.

First, it's the transition point between us and the outside world. On a practical level that can mean it becomes a drop zone for things like shoes, coats, backpacks, purses, keys, hats, umbrellas, dog leashes, piles of mail, etc.

At the same time, it's the first place we see when we come home and the first place anyone else sees when they come over.

The trick, then, is to create a space that is both functional and inviting.

I love this entry. A girl can dream! (Not mine.)

THE PATH IS CLEAR

TAKE AWAY

First, we need to make stepping inside easy and manageable. Start by clearing and cleaning every drawer and surface. Toss anything that can be easily tossed – junk mail, fading flowers, old batteries, and so on. Next, pick up anything that does not have a permanent home in the entry and return it to its rightful place – the kitchen, the kids' room, wherever.

RECONFIGURE

Eliminating, moving, or repositioning furniture and any other large pieces can make the space feel airier and more open, not to mention navigable. For the most part, any furniture in the entryway works best up against a wall, where it is not blocking any traffic.

ADD

Do you need a new welcome mat? Maybe a new hall runner? A water feature in the front yard, courtyard, or near the front door (table fountain) is something feng shui considers auspicious – a bearer of good fortune and abundance.

EASY DOES IT

For things that do have a permanent home in the entryway, it's time to create a system that adds to its functionality. Keys always in the same place? Check. Shoes corralled and findable? Check. Start by assessing what needs streamlining and how and where things tend to accumulate. Is it coats? Purses? Baseball caps? With this in mind, there are any number of things you can use to create a simple, functional, and attractive entry storage and organization system.

Mix and match any of the following:

- Hat and coat rack
- Shoe rack or boot tray for easily slipping off shoes
- Baskets or bins (can fill with socks and slippers)
- Console table
- Dresser
- Hutch
- Umbrella holder
- Storage bench
- Ottoman or settee
- Small bowl or bowls for things like keys, garage remotes, and coins (Security tip: keep in a drawer so as not to be visible.)
- Shelves
- Hooks
- Cubbies
- Pegboard
- Bookcase
- An "outgoing" basket or tote for things headed elsewhere – the dry cleaners, tailors, a friend's house, back to the store, even the car glove compartment or trunk

Within this, make sure you have a designated spot for mail, wherever that may be in the house. And, of course, deal with it in a timely manner so things don't stack up. Likewise, make sure you have a designated place for your purse, as you never want it to end up on the floor. There's an old saying, "Purse on the floor, money out the door."

A sidenote about shoes. I'm a big fan of not wearing them in the house. (Actually, I'm a big fan of not wearing them at all, but that's not the point.) For one thing, it cuts down on the tracking in of dirt and possible toxins from outside. Some people like having slippers or other "indoor shoes" they don't wear outside, often kept right by the front door. Personally, I go for being barefoot as much as possible.

The very first thing I ever heard my dear friend, the inimitable mindful movement coach and author extraordinaire Lawrence Biscontini, say, as he was teaching a yoga class, was that being barefoot is, "The way you were put on Earth." I loved that, and him, immediately.

In fact, you may be familiar with "earthing," the idea that we can enhance our wellbeing by walking barefoot on grass, sand, gravel, or dirt. Also known as grounding, the concept behind earthing says that walking sans shoes on natural substances puts us in direct contact with the electrical charges of planet Earth. Per healthline.com, this connection can help ease conditions such as fatigue, muscle pain, anxiety and depression, difficulty sleeping, and heart disease.

ELEGANT TIP

If you want to adopt a policy of no shoes in the house, keep extra pairs of slippers by the front door to offer guests.

CHEAP TRICK

When designing your entryway system, "shop" what you already own. What do you have that can be repurposed? Perhaps a bench for putting on or taking off shoes, some bowls or baskets for organizing keys or loose change, or a side table with drawers to keep things organized and out of sight.

ELEGANT TIP

Don't forget to have a plan for where to store purses, coats, and so on when friends visit. A hallway closet is great if you have one. A coat rack with enough available space is equally good, as are empty hooks on a wall. Even if all of these are generally full, clear some room temporarily to make guests feel welcome.

PUTTING STYLE IN FUNCTION

Once you've upgraded the functionality of the entry, the style becomes simple to uplevel. It doesn't require a major redo like a new paint job or renovation, although those are certainly options if you'd like and budget allows. What I'm talking about is playing around and getting creative with display. Think about making a statement with a special piece or two – a mirror, a beautiful rug, artwork, a photo gallery wall, mementos from your travels, or a prized family possession. As mentioned earlier, when you fill your home – especially the entry – with items like these, you're not just displaying things, you are displaying something about who you are and telling a bit of your story. Each piece helps you create a place that feels great to come home to, one that fills you with pride and tells you and your guests, "Welcome."

8.

LIVING ROOM – CREATING A SPOT WHERE PEOPLE *WANT* TO MEET UP

"What I really had was stories, the oral traditions of my parents. We moved so much that that was really our encyclopedia. A dream world told to me from my parents in the living room."

Juan Felipe Herrera (American Writer and U.S. Poet Laureate)

Many of us live in small spaces where the living room also functions as the dining room, office, and who knows what else. When I offer first-time guests the ten-cent tour of my house, I warn them that they are being severely overcharged. Then I say, "This is the dining room." I take two steps. "This is the living room." Another two steps. "This is the library."

Whether you have a tiny apartment in San Francisco or a great room in Miami, the living portion of the living room is a spot to unwind, relax, and connect with whomever you share your space with or invite over. It is where some of our favorite memories get made – of visiting and laughing with friends and family or doing a solo binge of your latest show.

And whether you call it a living room, family room, library, or den, this space is often the multitasker of the house. By any name, it is a gathering spot where you watch TV, snack, play games, read, and entertain people.

NOT THE METROPOLITAN – LIVED IN

While the living room is often the most formal room of the house, no one can relax in a place that feels uptight.

In her book *Homebody: A Guide to Creating Spaces You Never Want to Leave*, Joanna Gaines describes a time (before her Farmhouse and Magnolia days) she fell into the curating-like-a-museum trap and the need for the living room to look perfect at all times – even while her kids were playing in it! Her ah-ha moment came when she realized that level of perfection failed to reflect or say anything about the people living in the home.

In addition to representing who you are (individually and as a group) and what you hold dear, you want to make the living room functional for the ways you really use it, ways which make it feel cozy and inviting.

A FEW WAYS TO MAKE A LIVING ROOM FUNCTIONAL AND INVITING:

- A coffee table with a minimal number of things on it – leaving room for snacks or an indoor picnic, including plates, glasses, and mugs. As a sidenote, many coffee tables also offer storage – a win-win!
- Aim for a variety of textures, materials, and colors. Even with a mostly monochrome or neutral palette, throw pillows can add pops of color and texture and make the couch feel comfy and cozy. Extra points if you fluff them up.
- Scale counts. I've already mentioned how furniture must fit the room. A rug that is too small for the area will look like a postage stamp and make the room feel smaller. On the other hand, a rug that's too big will make your furniture look as if it is floating on an island. Best to use an area rug that reaches just under the main pieces to anchor the room.
- Keep it natural – plants, flowers, and nontoxic candles all add a nice something to a living room.
- A basket of blankets on hand for movie night. Alternatively, you can "store" folded blankets on the backs or arms of chairs and sofas.
- Baskets also work to store things like toys (for pets or kids).
- Boxes, bowls, dishes, and trays are great ways to keep things organized, out of sight, and easy to find.
- Consider not making the TV a focal point in the room. Cabinet doors and media cabinets are a great way to hide TVs when not in use.

- Make sure there is a designated spot for remotes – and that they get put back there (out of sight = out of sight).

- If the room gets used by lots of family members for lots of different purposes, assign everyone their own drawer, shelf, or cubby to minimize things getting confused, lost, or mislaid. Everyone will easily be able to find (and control) their own computers, papers, toys, and games.

- For the bookshelves, I organize books by type – biographies/memoirs, fiction, health, personal growth – so I can always find what I'm looking for. Taller books are laid flat, which adds visual interest.

- Toss any old magazines, catalogs, and books you're ready to part with. Get rid of any games or puzzles that are missing pieces or haven't been pulled out in over a year. If you're not quite ready to toss a certain game or puzzle, make a date to play it or use it. Then see if you still want to keep it.

- For a quick and relatively inexpensive refresh, you might repaint, reupholster, or add new hardware to couches, drawers, cabinets, etc. You'll be amazed at the big difference small upgrades make.

(A Puzzling) CHEAP TRICK

Leave a jigsaw puzzle out on a coffee or side table. You'll be surprised how everyone who walks in will stop for a second to fill in a piece. You might also be surprised at how often that second turns into hours…and fun conversation with whomever else has stopped by "for just a sec."

Fun for everyone.

ELEGANT TIP

Create an evening ritual everyone in the house can engage in to transition from a full day to a relaxed evening. At our place, the living room is where we gather for *Jeopardy!* and cocktails at the end of the day.

9.

BEDROOM – BETTER SLEEP, BETTER SEX

"Nothing messes with your erotic pleasure more than a messy bedroom. Get your bedroom flowing and your pleasure will flow right alongside it."

Sheila Kelley

(Actor, Founder, S Factor / sfactor.com, @sheilakelleys)

Ah, the sanctuary that is the bedroom. At least it should be. I mean, if you're getting your recommended hours of sleep each night, you spend about a third of your life there, as we've all heard a million times. And if you're going to spend a third of your life somewhere, it should darn well be a sanctuary – set up to support your sleep, your overall wellbeing, intimacy, and at least four of your five senses.

To wit:

- Looking Good: Aesthetically pleasing colors and textures, whatever that means to you, but definitely stick to soft, calming colors. Earth tones, light blues, lavenders, celadon greens, and pale yellows work well. Pastels are said to benefit relationships. White can feel clean and fresh. Red and orange tend to be too invigorating.

- Sounds Good: Earplugs, music, white/pink/brown noise machines (more on this in a minute), extra-thick curtains, properly sealed windows, as well as positioning furniture against the walls can all help block out street noise. If all else fails, soundproofing panels and/or double-glazed windows may be worth the investment.

- Like Buttah: Yummy, soft fabrics and textures, especially sheets.

- On The Nose: Smells clean and fresh.

CHEAP TRICK

Make your own room or pillow spray, or diffuser scent.

There are lots of room sprays, diffusers, and essential oils out there, but you want to be careful of the ingredients. Some of these contain things like formaldehyde and phthalates, to name just two super-gross things you don't want to be inhaling.

If you don't like the idea of a premade spray, you can make your own using an organic essential oil (lavender is calming, making it perfect for the bedroom) and water. Adding a few drops of vodka or witch hazel helps preserve it. Just pour it into a small, dark glass spritzer bottle and spritz away (clear glass will cause it to degrade too fast if exposed to light).

To use in a homemade diffuser, pour the mixture into a wide-mouth bud vase or small glass. Stir it with four to six wooden chopsticks. Reverse the chopsticks, leaving what has become the wet end sticking up. Voilà, an instant diffuser. Stir and repeat as desired.

(Note: These also work great in any other room in the house, especially the bathroom.)

The bedroom – according to rumor – should be used for only two things. I throw in reading, so it might be three.

That said, if you want your bedroom to be a sanctuary for sleeping, reading, and that other thing, then you need to set it up as such, which starts with the basics – declutter, clean up, put away, and organize.

One easy place to start – for the love of all things good and holy, get that pile of seventeen books off the nightstand! Yes, the one that feels like a huge, impossible to-do list sitting there mocking you. The Japanese even have a term for it: *tsundoku* (a combination of the words *tsumu*, meaning to pile up, and *doku*, meaning reading).

Put the books on a shelf or in a cabinet. They'll wait until you're actually ready to read them. Once you've tackled the top of the nightstand, move on to what's inside - toss outdated chargers, dried-out pens, and anything else you no longer use or is no longer in working order. A drawer tray is a great way to contain anything you put back, like (usable) pens, notepad, room spray, earbuds, or anything used during prayer or meditation (such as beads or crystals).

Fold, hang up, find a place for, or toss anything strewn on the floor or stowed under the bed. Messes like these can cause subconscious anxiety, affecting the quantity and quality of sleep. In fact, a study from St. Lawrence University (as reported by the American Academy of Sleep Medicine) found a correlation between excessive bedroom clutter and sleep disturbances. Furthermore, many feng shui experts believe that storing anything under the bed can upset sleep because energy (in this case, air) cannot flow easily and evenly around the bed. Around for about 6,00 years, feng shui is rooted in the idea that everything, including the items and décor in a room and how they are arranged, possesses energy that affects us. It further states that what is closest to us affects us most.

If real estate is at a premium and you have no choice but to store things under the bed, use clear, labeled bins so you can easily pull out what you need.

Another tip we've all heard time and again is to banish all electronics from the bedroom, including phones, tablets, computers, and even TVs. Blue light emissions tend to amp us up. EMFs are not healthy for us. Neither is being connected 24/7. Still, I'm a late and slow adopter here. For one thing, I like having my phone with me for safety and emergency reasons. Plus it's my alarm. So rather than beat myself up, I do what I can. I keep the TV in my bedroom hidden inside an armoire, which mitigates its impact, and I have an EMF shield on my phone which I hope helps offset my bad habits.

If your bedroom doubles as your office, make sure to turn off the computer at night and leave the desk area as tidied up as possible. Consider a decorative screen or curtain to divide the sleep and work portions of the room, at least at night. That will go a long way toward keeping the two areas separated, both physically and mentally.

MORNING

A good night starts with a good morning.

And a good morning starts with a good morning routine that inspires and supports you for the day ahead.

In the 200+ years since Benjamin Franklin wrote that he would "Rise, wash, and address Powerful Goodness" (as noted in ushistory. org), morning routines have been written about, debated, and become an obsession for some.

Among the things agreed to be supportive ways to set the intention and foundation for your day are:

- Journaling
- Meditating
- Praying
- Making a Gratitude List (a list of things for which you are grateful)
- Exercising
- Focusing on an inspirational or loved photo or piece of art
- Saying something nice to the first person you see
- Affirmations (saying something nice to yourself)
- Plain old smiling (especially if it's at yourself in the mirror)
- Drinking a glass of room-temperature water (As noted by realsimple.com, this helps rehydrate your body and wake up the digestive system. Cold water does not break down food as quickly.)

Furthermore, according to the law of attraction (the idea that "like attracts like"), anything you do to become more mindful, make yourself feel present, and express gratitude – for yourself, for others, for your situation – will naturally attract more of those things to you throughout the day. We can all find something.

Mel Robbins wrote an entire book, *The High 5 Habit*, about the power of giving yourself a "high 5" in the mirror first thing each day. A high 5 is a celebration and means you did something right – even if it is just getting out of bed. Speaking of which…

MAKE YOUR BED

It may seem like such a little thing but making the bed matters. For one thing, you start your day having accomplished something. For another, it makes the room not only look better but feel better, especially if you let the sheets air out a bit first. Because (as I've stated before and probably will again before we're done), whether you realize it or not, a messy space affects you psychologically, dragging you down and sapping you of energy. And making the bed every morning can rub off into other areas of your life, making you more likely to feel – and be – more organized, more productive, and less stressed all around. It also shows respect, for yourself and for your things. As an additional note, I always feel the change in energy in my room when the sheets are freshly washed.

That said, I used to really, really not care about hospital corners. I didn't see all the fuss, as I couldn't figure out what they accomplished. Do they actually keep sheets in place any better? Do they make sleeping any easier? Will anyone ever see them? No. No. And no. Full disclosure, I am absolutely useless at making hospital corners. However, I have started to come around and now actually see the benefit of having a "properly" made bed, even if it's just an increased sense of accomplishment and elegance. So, I am practicing my tucking and folding over.

A made bed – accomplishment #1 for the day!

CHEAP TRICK

Fitted sheets can tend to slip and ride up. There are lots of items you can get cheaply and easily to keep them in place – from foam grippers (be warned, they can disintegrate after a while) to mattress straps to clip-on sheet straps.

LET THE SUN SHINE

For an extra dose of good juju, open any bedroom blinds, shutters, or curtains, as well as windows. A bit of sunshine and fresh air will help the room feel fresh and clean, and may even brighten your mood.

What's more, getting a little light exposure helps set our circadian rhythm, signaling to our brains that it's day/awake time vs. evening/wind-down time. Stanford University professor Andrew Huberman (scopeblog.stanford.edu) further recommends that we all go outside to get sunlight in our eyes first thing upon waking. Even if it's cloudy, it helps to set your biological clock, triggering a neural circuit that controls the timing of the releasing of cortisol and melatonin, hormones that affect sleep. If it's warm enough, I sometimes take my coffee out to the patio for a few minutes first thing in the a.m.

Exposure to natural light can also keep us more energized throughout the day.

Coffee on the patio.

WHERE DOES THIS THING GO?

A few notes regarding how to position the bed, courtesy of feng shui:

- It should view the doorway but not be in direct line with the door. This is called the "command position" and allows you to feel safer than if you couldn't see the door and had a subconscious need to "keep an eye out" for anyone trying to enter.
- It should not be directly under a window because, again, this can make you feel vulnerable to outside forces.
- It should not have heavy art hanging above it. No matter how securely it is hung, this puts you on subconscious alert, as if it might come crashing down on you. Choose lighter-weight pieces and make sure they feature a calm or romantic image to up the intimacy factor.

- If possible, have open space on both sides of the bed, as well as a lamp and nightstand on both sides. This creates a sense of symmetry which, in turn, creates a sense of balance in the relationship with whomever you are sharing the room…and bed. Even if you don't have a current partner, this can help create space for a future love.
- Headboards help create a sense of security and calm.

WHEN THE WHEN MATTERS

Sleep is one of the most important things we can do for our health. It's when our entire system (physical and mental) detoxes and resets. And it's free!

Indeed, there is a ton of research on how sleep, or lack thereof, affects our health.

But, first, does it matter WHEN we sleep?

Ayurveda and Traditional Chinese Medicine (TCM), among other schools of thought, say our bodies are timed to follow day and night. They say the best hours for sleep are from roughly 10:00 p.m. to 6:00 a.m. Furthermore, some evidence even suggests that getting into bed after 12:00 a.m. can lead not just to the dreaded second wind, but to psychological issues over time, such as depression and Seasonal Affective Disorder (SAD). This is possibly because you're now getting out of bed later in the day and missing out on some of that great early morning sunshine. It might also be related to the altered length of time you are exposed to the one REM (rapid eye movement) and three non-REM sleep cycles each night, which have been shown to happen at about the same hours no matter when you fall asleep. This is important because of the different functions each of these cycles plays. While each is said to last about 90 minutes, REM sleep is when we dream and consolidate memories. Non-REM sleep is deeper and more restorative.

On the other hand, chronotypes take into account your natural tendency, in short are you a biological "early bird" or "night owl." Each of the four chronotypes thrives under different conditions in terms of when they sleep and for how long. Lions like to get up early and have a medium sleep drive. Bears like a lot of sleep and tend to follow the solar cycle. Wolves love to stay up late. Dolphins are often tired during the day while wired and restless at night (per Psychology Today).

And while chronotypes are influenced by genetic predispositions, sleep needs change as we change – personal preference, lifestyle (including diet, exercise, and schedules), as well as health concerns all evolve as we do.

SLEEP AND HEALTH

The latest studies show there is no single magic number or one-size-fits-all to the amount of sleep you should be getting each night. Everyone has their own sweet spot of how much shuteye they need on a consistent (read: nightly) basis, generally between 6.5 and 9 hours a night, depending on things like age and genetics. The important thing is getting quality sleep during those hours and allowing your body to go through all of the sleep cycles.

Before we get into the havoc too little sleep can wreak on your health, know that it's absolutely possible to get too much sleep.

Zoma Sleep conducted a study in which they looked at the average sleep time in 37 countries. They factored in the health grade of each country using the Bloomberg Healthiest Country Index, along with the life expectancy in each country. They found that Spain has the world's highest health grade (97.25), while Japan has the highest life expectancy (84.2 years). The average Spaniard gets 436 minutes of sleep each night, the average person in Japan gets 433. Mexico, the country with the lowest life expectancy and second-to-lowest health grade, has the highest average sleep time at 540 minutes each night.

While people in the U. S. sleep about the same amount of time as Spain and Japan (430 minutes), it ranks 30th for health grade and 28th for life expectancy. Obviously, many lifestyle factors (stress and diet among them) affect our overall health, not just sleep.

Of course, no matter how many hours you spend trying to get some shuteye, if you aren't actually dozing off, you aren't getting much benefit from being in the sack. So, what are some of the health problems related to not getting enough *quality* sleep?

There is not one organ or bodily system which is not affected when we are sleep-deprived, but here is a short list of some of the effects:

- Reduced creativity
- Reduced productivity
- Motor skill impairment
- Poor digestion
- Slowed cell regeneration
- Weight issues
- High blood pressure
- Increased risk for diabetes (sleep helps stabilize blood sugar)
- Risk of falling/poor balance
- Risk of heart disease (sleep boosts cardiovascular health)
- Inability to focus or stay awake during the day
- Memory loss
- Chronic inflammation
- Decreased immunity
- Increased irritability

- Depression
- Anxiety
- Increased risk of car accidents
- Lower fertility in both men and women
- Lowered sex drive

YOU GOTTA HAVE HEART

Heart disease is now the number one killer worldwide. Period. When it comes specifically to the heart, both when you go to sleep and how much quality sleep you get matter.

Researchers at the European Society of Cardiology found that people who fall asleep between 10:00 p.m. and 11:00 p.m. may be less likely to develop cardiovascular disease than those who go to bed earlier or later.

Another study, from the *Journal of Clinical Sleep Medicine*, suggests the importance of considering sleep duration and sleep quality together when developing strategies to improve sleep for cardiovascular disease prevention.

A "SLEEP DIVORCE"?

Sounds like a bad thing, but it could do wonders! You really do have to figure out what works for you – and then adjust your space and lifestyle to support it. Even if this means going to bed at a different time, or in a different room, from your significant other, you might be a more present, happier, and overall better partner to them – and parent to your kids if you have them – when you are together.

THAT'S GOTTA HURT

Need even more evidence that good sleep matters? Ask Arianna Huffington. In 2007 she passed out from exhaustion at her desk, breaking her cheekbone. This event taught her an important lesson: success does NOT equal burning the candle at both ends at the expense of your health. Do not wear that as a badge of honor. It isn't one. Lesson learned and cheek healed, Arianna transformed into a self-described "sleep evangelist," literally writing the book on good sleep, *The Sleep Revolution.*

Writing for wellandgood.com, she also touts the importance of the transition from daytime to bedtime (AKA a nighttime routine), saying that walking through the bedroom door should put an end to all problems of the day, at least temporarily.

In other words, whatever the issue, you can think about it tomorrow à la Scarlett O'Hara – maybe with new solutions having been formed by the sleep committee or a clearer head. Of course, if your mind is racing, just turning it off is easier said than done, so here are a few tried and true tips for how to unwind and leave the day behind, to help you experience the ultimate "bedgasm" (the euphoria of falling into bed at the end of a full day).

While my personal nighttime routine mostly consists of a very short list-making (to-dos and meetings/appointments for the next day) and journaling session, followed by "brush teeth, wash face, apply products," here are a few ideas you can incorporate if you have a bit of trouble transitioning from awake to asleep:

- Write down your to-do list for the next day so it doesn't plague you during the night. A Baylor University study found that students who wrote down tasks to be completed were able to fall asleep significantly faster than students who wrote down tasks they had already finished. Furthermore, the more detailed the to-do list, the faster they fell asleep.
- Visualize how you want the next day to go.
- Write down three things you are grateful for from the day, or in your life in general.
- Meditate, perhaps with the help of a meditation sleep app.
- Create a dark space (an eye mask works nicely or consider blackout shades if they might help).
- Take a bath (Epsom salts help soothe muscles).
- Drink some tea (caffeine free).
- Jujube, either as a fruit or tea, is said to enhance sleep quality.
- Pop a magnesium supplement.
- White noise machine: According to mindbodygreen.com, most white noise machines actually play a variety of "colors." White noise sounds like static or a whirring fan and works at drowning out other noise but may be a bit "amping." Most people do best with pink and brown frequencies, which are lower than white. Pink sounds like waves on a beach or rustling leaves. Brown sounds like low roaring or heavy rainfall.
- Use earplugs.
- Use pillow or room spray.
- Wear socks if it's cold. We've all heard the phrase "cold feet" in connection with having second thoughts. It's really just about having thoughts at all. Because when our feet are cold our mind starts to race all over the place.

- Per the Sleep Foundation, weighted blankets are said to ease stress, calm the nervous system, and increase the production of serotonin, the mood-boosting hormone. They may also decrease the production of cortisol, the stress hormone.

- Turn off lamps that emit white or full-spectrum light at sundown. Opt instead for salt lamps and amber bulbs to mimic the natural world.

- Know when to say when to streaming – don't get a second wind by binging too late.

- Minimize or ban electronics in the bedroom. A constant state of being connected does not support disconnecting. And decreasing your exposure to EMFs (electromagnetic frequencies) couldn't hurt, although there is a lot of conflicting information about the type of and exposure level to EMFs and what to be concerned about.

- Cut out the blue light from scrolling at least forty-five minutes before sleep time. If you can't cut down the time, blue-light-blocking computer glasses or amber goggles can help lessen the amount of blue light you are exposed to. So do blue light blocking screens you can attach right on to your phone or computer.

- If you do watch something, try an ASMR video. (No, it's not porn! ASMR stands for Autonomous Meridian Sensory Response.) ASMR videos are full of soothing sounds and visuals meant to trigger a relaxing, tingly sensation in you.

- Read a book. This piece of advice is backed by research, just be sure it is a physical book. Again, devices give off too much blue light, which is stimulating.

- Do a crossword puzzle.

- Sing or hum something soft and soothing – maybe a lullaby from your childhood.
- Maintain a clean, clutter-free bedroom.
- Don't sleep in workout clothes. Apparently, some people actually do this. Hello? This is a thing? I get that it is meant to save time in the morning, but it sends the completely wrong message to your brain, telling it that it's time to work out, not check out. Leave your workout clothes ready to go in the a.m. and stick to your favorite sleep-time pieces for bed.

BEAUTY SLEEP

Looking to turn sleep time into *beauty* sleep time? Here are some ideas:

- Never go to bed without washing off every trace of makeup.
- Silk or satin pillowcases can be a game changer. They are kinder to your skin, causing fewer wrinkles and eliminating the dreaded morning pillow crease face. They also don't soak up all those products you bothered to slather on before turning in. Furthermore, they don't pull at or break hair or cause frizzies. There are lots of affordable silk and satin pillowcases out there. Get thee some. Change often to reduce the bacteria your face comes in contact with when using any pillowcase night after night. Helps avoid breakouts.
- Gloves and lotion at bedtime make for uber-soft hands come morning time.
- Ditto for socks and lotion on feet.

- A breast pillow. A what??? Yep, it's a thing. Basically, it's this very padded contraption with both vertical and horizontal adjustable straps which you wear while sleeping, over your pajamas. And I swear it is not the least bit uncomfortable. Now, why in the world would you want one? It helps to reduce wrinkles in the décolletage and between the ole breasts. I got mine to help minimize a surgery scar.

ELEGANT TIP 1

Buy organic, nontoxic sheets, mattress, and pillows if you can swing them. Cotton is the most popular fabric for sheets, but most cotton is grown using pesticides. Bamboo, another popular material for sheets, requires chemicals to break down the fibers into something usable. And, if by any chance you dry clean your sheets (I know someone who does), please use an organic dry cleaner. You don't want to be sleeping with toxic chemicals.

ELEGANT TIP 2

If you've ever driven yourself crazy trying to get a duvet back into a duvet cover, my bedmaking was made 100x easier when I discovered that many duvets come with a loop of fabric in each corner and many duvet covers come with a set of strings in each corner. Just tie the strings through the loops and – voilà – the whole task becomes sooo much easier.

BOTTOM LINE

No matter the specific issue, getting adequate quality sleep makes you healthier both physically and mentally. Emotionally, it improves your attitude and outlook, making you cheerier and more pleasant to be around. (Nobody enjoys a crankoid!)

Simply put, sleep is key to living a healthy life – in quality and quantity.

And for those who still think this whole third of your life thing is a waste of time, consider this – Albert Einstein supposedly slept ten hours a night. We know how that worked out. Inventor Nikola Tesla was pretty impressive himself. But he apparently thought sleep was a waste of time and averaged just two hours a night, which may have aggravated a list of mental health issues he suffered from, including OCD. And take note, some say he also thought sex was a waste of time, though he reportedly never tried it.

10.

CLOSET – FULL OF WHAT TO WEAR, NOT JUST FULL OF CLOTHES

"Your closet needs to be a place of joy and celebration of who you are now – not who you were."

Stacy London (Stylist and Fashion Consultant, CEO, State of Menopause / @stacylondonreal)

O CLOSET! MY CLOSET!

What West Los Angeles girl doesn't love her some clothes? This one sure does. As a young kid, I loved dressing and creating "unexpected" combinations - plaids with polka dots, purple with green. So much so, I sometimes changed my outfit five or six times a day, leaving the barely worn clothes strewn all over the floor.

Today, I still love clothes and how they can change your attitude, but I generally manage with one ensemble a day (outside of workout wear and PJs). At its best, clothing can make you feel sexy, cozy, confident, playful, or empowered. I love fashion as self-expression. I love seeing people dress in the best, most authentic expression of themselves.

Which means I would *never* make suggestions for a "capsule" wardrobe. In fact, I hate the very idea of a capsule wardrobe. Too prescriptive, too restrictive. (You need one white button-down blouse, one black pair of pants? Puh-lease!) Where is the fun? Where is the play? Where is the creativity? Where is the spontaneity? Where is the dressing up to highlight a certain aspect of yourself or for attending a certain event?

Besides, I don't know you, your lifestyle, your coloring, or your body type. I have no idea what shapes, textures, and colors are flattering on you. So I would never presume to prescribe any cut-and-dried rules. (Sidenote: No, black is NOT universally flattering. I look horrible in it and, as such, my "little black dress" is, in fact, navy.)

Clothing (read: fashion) is meant to be fun. It is meant to be beautiful (in the eyes of the wearer), creative, and allow us to express a unique part of ourselves.

MOVE THE ENERGY

It's often the people with the most clothes who feel they have "nothing to wear." Paradoxically, owning fewer things can make getting dressed much easier. That's because a full closet is full of stuck energy and visual noise, making it hard to see what you have in there. Meaning…

A pared-down and organized closet is a time-saving closet.

And it can actually make it seem as though you have more clothes, not fewer, as it offers increased clarity around what you own and how to mix and match it all with ease and creativity. With that in mind, here are a few specific tips for keeping your wardrobe fun and functional, while prioritizing the pieces which make you feel comfortable and fashionable.

Nicely organized!

CURATE LIKE A NINJA

- Once again, empty every drawer and closet with the intention of deciding what to keep, as opposed to what to get rid of. Only put back what you love, what makes you feel your best, what reflects the you that you are now, and what fits in the space. Everything else goes. OK, if you *really* have a lot of clothes, you may want to do this by category. But do try to get everything *in* a category out at once, as it will give you a better idea of what you actually have. And knowing what you have makes it easier to decide what to keep because you will be less likely to hold on to a particular item "just in case."

- Make sure everything you keep fits both you (your body) and your lifestyle.

- Destination does not apply to clothing. If you're holding on to clothes that don't fit because someday you might be able to squeeze into that size (insert number here), get rid of them. They only take up real estate and serve to mock, not inspire, you. Of course, there are exceptions to every rule: If you are pregnant, if you are recovering from injury or surgery, if your weight naturally fluctuates regularly, these are all things to take into consideration. Still, it's a good idea to get most clothes you're not currently using out of the closet. This may be the one time to store them until you can use them.

- Questions to ask yourself when curating a wardrobe:
  - Why do I own this?
  - What purpose does it serve?
  - When is the last time I wore it, regardless of how much I love it in theory? (One school of thought says if you haven't worn

it in the last 12 months, you're not going to wear it in the next 12 months.)

- Do I like the fit and the way it falls on me?
- Does the cut flatter me?
- Does the color flatter me?
- Do I like the texture and does it work for me? (Some people can handle heavier textures, others can't.)
- Is it good quality?
- How do I feel in it?
- Do I love it?
- Would I buy it again?
- Is it ME?

- Make a pile of things that need mending, such as split seams or missing buttons.
- Anything that has holes, worn-out elastic, or stains can be let go, no guilt required.
- Have fun giving away, donating, or selling what you aren't keeping. Many apps make it super easy to make a little money (perhaps for a future investment piece).
- Host a wardrobe swap with your best pals.
- The 80/20 Rule of Clothing. I am willing to bet you have more clothes than you need. How do I know? The 80/20 Rule. Simply put, that means you wear 20% of the clothes you own 80% of the time. (Am I right?) So what about the rest? Do you really love/need/wear them (at least sometimes)?
- My father was a believer in "replace only," also known as the "One in, One out" Rule. Meaning, if space is a concern, don't buy anything new, such as shoes, until an old pair has worn out, freeing up a place to put them.

- All of the above holds true not just for clothes and outerwear, but for accessories as well – purses, jewelry, belts, hats, scarves, etc.
- Always have a bin, box, shelf, or bag as a designated place for putting anything ready to go to the donation center or online to sell.

ORGANIZE LIKE A PRO

- Choose one style of hanger – thin and streamlined, not wide and bulky, especially if space is at a premium. I cannot begin to tell you what a difference this makes in creating space in your closet. I used to have lovely, bulky wooden hangers. Then I switched to lovely, thin velvet hangers. My closet grew by 25%, I swear. Clothes can slip off plastic hangers, velvet is kinder on fabrics. Dry cleaner hangers are flimsy and unattractive.
- I have a special section at the front of my closet where empty hangers go. This keeps the rest of the closet looking neat, organized, and streamlined.
- Arrange clothes by type (shirts, pants, jackets) and color (light to dark). Place everything facing the same direction.
- I have found it helpful to separate my sweatpants and joggers from the rest of my slacks. That way, I'm not forced to wade through tons of pieces that aren't what I'm looking for.
- Bye-bye, tags. Once you buy something new, remove the tags before putting it away. Makes for less mess.
- If you keep shoes in shoe boxes, stick a picture of the pair to the outside of the box to make it easy to grab the one you want.

- For many of us (hand raised), working out can cost "activation energy." In other words, we won't do it if it's too hard to get ready. So, we need to make it easy on ourselves. For me, that means having one special place with easy access to my workout gear – bras, baseball cap, and especially shoes (which, when stored in the back of my closet equals too much trouble to dig out).
- There are tons of systems out there for organizing everything from socks to tank tops to shoes to baseball caps and purses. Find a system which works for you.

MAINTAIN THAT INVESTMENT

- Tailors are everyone's best friend. The difference between a piece of clothing that looks great (high quality and expensive, no matter the actual price) and one that doesn't? Fit. A tailored piece can be the difference between looking elegant and looking schlubby. As the saying goes, "If you don't have fit, you don't have anything." I'm not – oh, what's the word...tall? So for me, my tailor takes in everything – hem lengths, shoulders, sleeves, and even necklines on occasion. (Thank you, Kim.) Caveat: the hardest thing to alter is shoulders, so if an item is too wide there it might not be worth buying in the first place. You may also find that your tailor can help mend things like rips and holes in items you don't want to let go.
- When storing clothes in garment bags, cloth is definitely the way to go. Clothes need to breathe. Plastic can cause discoloration and deterioration of the fabric, as well as mold from trapped moisture.

Also:

- For giving clothes that nice, pressed look, I like handheld steamers better than irons. I think they're easier to use and take up less room when not in use.
- Fabric shavers can help get rid of the pills that tend to accumulate on sweaters, saving them from looking old and worn out.

CHEAP TRICK

Clothing moths feed on natural fibers – hair, wool, silk, cashmere, cotton – especially when dirty. To keep them at bay, first, keep your clothes clean! Brushing jackets or coats, anything you don't need to clean as often, can really extend their life and keep them from attracting clothes pests. Try cedar, lavender, peppermint, chrysanthemum, rosemary, thyme, or lilac sachets or treated wood pieces as an added deterrent. These can be easily freshened up with organic essential oil. Or be crafty and make a homemade pomander ball by sticking whole cloves through the skin of an orange until the orange is completely covered. Hang it by a ribbon in your closet. Smells divine – to us humans, not so much to moths.

Whatever you use, stay away from traditional mothballs made of naphthalene or paradichlorobenzene, as both are highly toxic pesticides whose fumes we inhale. Side effects can include anemia, kidney and liver damage, and a host of other problems of varying severity (per the Louisiana Department of Health and Hospitals).

SOME INCONVENIENT TRUTHS

Elegant or cozy, clothing comes at a cost. And I don't mean the price tag. I'm talking about both the human and environmental toll of producing fashion, especially "fast fashion" – clothing that is trendy, quick and cheap to produce, and not meant to last.

Let's start with the human toll. Despite gains made in the area, sweatshops do exist – where laborers are forced to work in horrid conditions, often with little air, locked doors, and exposure to chemicals. Some of these laborers are children. I'll never forget the time I bought a T-shirt off a pile at a very fast fashion store. When I got it home, I realized the buttons at the top of the neck were sewn in a crooked line. All I could think about was some poor child laborer. How do you guard against this? Research the practices of the companies you buy from and beware of a couple of traps. First of all, just because a celebrity slaps their name on a line of clothing, it doesn't mean they have even the vaguest idea of where or how those items are being made. Secondly, even if clothes are manufactured in the U.S., you still cannot be 100% sure of the company's labor practices.

As for the environment, just remember that the fashion industry "contributes" to deforestation, the use of chemicals and pesticides (in the case of nonorganic fabrics), and tremendous water use (including possible illegal dumping of wastewater).

The good news is that many companies are becoming more transparent about their material and labor practices.

SHOP LIKE A GURU

Shopping intentionally is all about being strategic, making conscious and conscientious choices about what you purchase.

Concentrating on new pieces to become part of the 20% you wear 80% of the time will give you the most bang for your buck.

But first, before shopping, shop your own closet. It can be fun to play stylist with stuff you already own, rather than buying something new.

- Get creative with putting together new outfit combinations.
- Wear something you haven't put on in a while.
- Really consider if you actually need to purchase anything new or if you have plenty of things with plenty of wear left in them. If there is a look or trend you've noticed, see if you can create your own version with things you already own.
- Spending your money on things for "someday" doesn't make sense. You may be dreaming of that safari in Africa or that walk on the beach in Cozumel, but if you don't have it on your calendar, don't shop for it. By the time you do schedule it, trends, your taste, and your body may have changed.

ELEGANT TIP

Quality, not quantity – better to spend a bit more on fewer things that will last longer. But first, define your style. Be selective about the trends you participate in, making sure they suit you. It's often better to think timeless, not trendy. What will you wear for years, not just this year? How can you tell good quality? Shop with your hands - the feel and texture of the material will tell you everything you need to know. Is it soft? Is it breathable? Is the construction sturdy?

IT'S WINE O'CLOCK – STEP AWAY FROM THE CART

I'll share a little something online retailers know but won't tell. At nine o'clock, once the kitchen is cleaned up (and perhaps the kids are in bed) and you're having an extra glass of Chardonnay, your online cart tends to fill up, meaning your bank account tends to empty. One easy tip? Step away. Leave the goodies in the cart until tomorrow, when you can decide with fresh eyes if they're really something you want to invest in. This will save you from unwanted clothes, unnecessary returns, and fluctuating credit card balances. Oh my!

REDUCE, REUSE, RECYCLE

We've already discussed reducing the number of things you buy, now think about reusing. Here are a few tips:

- Revamp and rethink the clothes you are keeping. Can you breathe new life into something by tailoring it? Cutting it up (e.g., turning pants into shorts)? Adding new details or changing out the buttons? This can change an item's purpose in your wardrobe, making it more classic, modern, formal, or casual.
- Buy secondhand at a donation store or online. (Hey, it's new to you!)
- Wear an outfit again and again. Even if you've "been seen" in it. No one will remember. Actress Shirley MacLaine wore the same dress to the Oscars® two years in a row.

As for recycling, it's not that easy. Not many municipalities offer textile recycling and almost all of the retailers that did have since dropped their programs. So the sad news is that most discarded clothing ends up in landfill. Very little of it is made into new fabric.

In the end, closets and wardrobes are always a work in progress. If you're not quite ready to get rid of that prom dress or Elvis sweatshirt, no worries. Listen to that inner voice.

11.

BATHROOM – CREATING AN AT-HOME SPA

"There is no cosmetic for beauty like happiness."

Maria Mitchell (American Astronomer)

To me, the bathroom is a sanctuary, a place that calms and centers, a place where we perform the rituals of getting ready – for the day, for a party, for bed. A ritual in this sense means doing something mindfully and with intention. Rituals take a routine to the next level. That's what I love to do in the bathroom, take that extra moment to enjoy the water splashing on my face as I wash it, to smell the oil I pour in the bath, to feel the silkiness of the serum I'm applying, making sure it gets warmed between my palms for maximum absorption. When we're engaged in doing these types of things, we're not on our phone, computer, or doing something for someone else. Special moments are created when we are honoring ourselves by being present.

What does this have to do with decluttering, with making things simpler and more elegant? I'll tell you.

When we engage in the above-mentioned rituals,
we are focusing on ourselves, figuratively decluttering
the mind, which is hard to do
if we are surrounded by actual clutter.

PRETTY IS AS PRETTY DOES

I used to be somewhat of a beauty junkie. My fascination/obsession with products was cemented when I worked as a producer on *Glow*, a TV series for E! Networks dedicated to all things beauty – the latest topical fixes, this season's makeup colors, and trends for tresses and nails. If it was happening in the beauty world, we were on it. As an extra perk, brands would send us products to consider featuring. About once a month all this SWAG was piled onto the conference room table for the grabbing. Talk about hog heaven!

But junkie ways can get out of hand, leading to shelves, drawers, and cabinets crammed with ten-step systems, hotel-sized lotions and body wash, and way too many red lipsticks.

Yep, that was my bathroom – every available inch filled to the brim with the latest items promising miracle cures for the face, body, hair, teeth, you name it.

Then I had four realizations:

- A whole lot of these products (OK, most!) did not deliver said miracle.
- I was spending a whole lot of money on this nonexistent holy grail - even with all the free stuff.

- Less is more. My skin is too sensitive and reactive to be slathering on layer after layer of product. It seems to me that the fewer products you use on your face, the less likely you are to get clogged pores, breakouts, and general irritation, and the more likely it is that what you do put on your face will be absorbed and, therefore, effective.
- I just like the way my bathroom looks and functions with fewer products crammed into every nook and cranny.

I love this look - and the just-right number of products.

So, as with every room in the house, step one is to purge what you don't need, use, or love. Empty every space housing all your bathroom goodies:

- Get rid of the pink blush that you know doesn't work for you.
- Ditch the over-fragranced hand soap you've never been able to bring yourself to use.

- Feel free to throw in – make that throw out – anything expired, which will usually look a little off in color and smell a little off in scent. Also check the date, most products are formulated to last anywhere from six months to two years.
- And, of course, double-check for anything that is hanging around empty.

Step two is organizing your vanity, counter, drawers, medicine cabinet, and/or shelves. Woven baskets, bins, jars, makeup organizers, toiletry turntables, and tissue holders all help to keep things in place while being pretty and creating a look.

The biggest game changer for me was adding drawer organizers to the drawers in my bathroom.

Finally, the bathroom is one of the two places (the other being the office) where I am a fan of stocking up. It always helps to keep multiples/backups of things like toothbrushes, shampoo, razors, sunscreen, etc. You never want to run out and be stuck.

KEEPING THINGS SUSTAINABLE

Often, a huge portion of the cost of beauty products is the fancy packaging. Buying things with minimal packaging not only saves you money, it saves you time opening and unwrapping said packaging, and, of course, it creates less waste, thus helping save the planet. I also discard the packaging it does come in the minute it gets in the house. Even if I'm not ready to use it yet, it takes up less space in the drawer or on the shelf.

Swap out single-use items like sheet masks, makeup remover cloths, and cotton pads for reusable, washable alternatives. Eco- and wallet-friendly.

CHEAP TRICK

Look no further than your kitchen staples and scraps to save even more money and space on all sorts of beauty products.

- Bananas (even just the inside of the peels), pumpkin puree, avocados, and honey all make great moisturizing masks for the face.

- Egg whites create a firming mask and, when paired with honey and/or lemon, reduce oil and bacteria on the face.

- Finely ground oatmeal or cornmeal can become a gentle exfoliator.

- Raw apple cider vinegar works as a toner to balance the pH level of the skin.

- Olive oil, eggs, and mayonnaise (solo or in any combination) guarantee incredibly soft locks when used to condition hair before washing.

SHOWER TIME

I love going for a spa day. So fun. So relaxing. Also so far away from my house and so expensive! It's actually super-easy to create a spa-like shower experience at home, complete with beautiful smells, heavenly oils, and plush robe.

- Many people recommend beginning with dry brushing, which helps drain the lymphatic system (a form of flushing toxins from the body) and sloughs off dead skin before you even step into the water. A lot of people (by which I mean me) find dry brushing scratchy and unpleasant. At the very least it may take some getting used to. Alternatively, you can do an exfoliating body scrub in the shower once a week. It feels great and leaves your skin smooth as well as moisturized from all the oil in the scrub.

- Indulge in *abhyanga*, the Ayurvedic term for self-massage using warm oil. (Jojoba oil is a good bet as it works for all of the Ayurvedic "doshas," or physical constitutions.) Just warm up some oil, slowly massage all over and relax for five to fifteen minutes before getting in the shower. You may want to avoid being too vigorous with washing it off, as leaving some oil behind will leave your skin nice and soft.

- Turn your shower into a real spa experience by placing a few drops of essential oil onto the shower floor. Be sure to sprinkle it far enough away from you that you don't need to worry about the floor becoming slippery. Breathe in and enjoy. For an even bigger oomph, you can buy an herb bundle for the shower. They smell amazing – when the shower is not on and even more when it is – but they do take up a bit of space and require periodic replacing. Other options include shower melts, shower sprays, and frozen orange peels thrown on the shower floor.

- Sing! Belting out some tunes is a great stress reliever.
- A pumice does a great job of getting the rough bits off your feet.
- For the smoothest shave on your legs, start by running the razor down the leg, then up.
- Brrr!!! Finishing your shower with a cold blast (work your way up to three minutes) may boost immunity, decrease inflammation, improve both circulation and mood, and even up metabolism by activating brown fat (adipose tissue stored around the shoulders and neck) and balancing certain hormone levels. At the very least, it'll wake you up. (Other options for this include investing in a plunge pool or going for Cryotherapy sessions. But please note that the Cleveland Clinic warns against all of these for people with heart disease or those who are prone to arrhythmia.)
- For super-soft skin once you get out of the shower, ditch the towel completely. Instead, pour on a bit of body oil (if you haven't already done *abhyanga*) and wrap yourself in a nice plush robe without drying off. Your skin will become extra touchable. (Note: Make sure your robe is pure terry cloth. It can stand up to the oil without staining and can easily go in the wash.)

A BATH CAN DO WHAT?

From bubbles to rubber duckies, a bath can be romantic (à deux), fun, restorative, luxurious and indulgent, calming, or help bring forth creative ideas.

Salt can do wonders for a bath. Epsom salts help ease sore muscles. Sea salt is said to help clear negative energy. Just don't try to mix salt with bubbles as it dissolves the lovely foam.

And let's not forget the oils. Pouring a few drops of your favorite oil into the bath water will ensure you come out with impossibly soft skin.

If you want to extend your soak for as long as possible, be sure to use a tub plug. I have two – one goes over the drain and one covers the flip lever. Add a bath pillow, lie back, and be "taken away."

ELEGANT TIP

On a chilly winter morning, throw your robe (or towel) in the dryer. Leave for a couple of minutes, then grab it before heading to the shower or bath. It will still be toasty when you get out.

ELEGANCE – PERFUME

While it may seem like a small thing, nothing screams elegant self-care like taking a few seconds to apply some perfume. Whether you love to mix it up or are loyal to one scent, here are a few things to remember when you spray or roll it on:

- The perfect time to apply scent is right after a shower or bath.
- Spray you, not your clothes – skin and clothes are not made of the same material, so spraying clothes won't get you the same results, as perfume is formulated to work with skin. Plus perfume may stain some fabrics.
- Spray on pulse points (wrists, elbows, knees), cleavage, and hair to warm it up and release the fullest scent. If you want a lighter hint of fragrance, spritz the air in front of you and step into the fragrance as it rains down.
- "Don't bruise our creations." That quote is from a master perfumer interviewed on my old TV show *Glow*. He was referring to rubbing your wrists together after spraying them. This "crushes" the ingredients in the perfume.

THE ????: SETTLING THE DEBATE ONCE AND FOR ALL

OK, I feel so strongly about this one that I don't understand why it is even a debate. But, apparently, it is. So here are my two cents worth about…the toilet seat.

Should it be left up to accommodate standing users or down for the ease of seated users?

Final answer is…*NEITHER.*

The lid should always be put down after every use, closing the toilet (so to speak). Not only is this much more pleasing to the eye, but it guards against the feng shui concept of allowing your money to go down the drain. So, in short, keep a lid on it. 'Nuff said.

Finally, I am not a fan of using the back of the toilet as storage space. It's kinda gross and looks icky, if you ask me. You can always install a small glass shelf just above the toilet for extra storage space if need be.

12.

KIDS' ROOMS – LET THEM READ BOOKS! (OR PLAY GAMES OR...)

"Play is the work of childhood."

Maria Montessori (Italian Physician and Educator)

"No Adults Allowed." That was the sign on my bedroom door when I was a kid. It wasn't that adults weren't actually welcomed. It reflected what I think all kids want – agency and a place to call their own, a place where they call the shots and can do what they want to do. A place for them just to be them is critical for developing a sense of self, a sense of self-reliance, and a sense of what lights them up.

ELEGANT TIP

This one is about the beauty of leaning into authenticity. If you've got kids, you've got a mess – with any luck, one that is relatively confined to designated spaces. That said, lean into the joy of letting your kids grow and explore their world. Lean into the ease of not needing things to look perfect.

Still, you can certainly help kids stay on top of their clutter. Get them excited about the process of creating and maintaining spaces. Use it as a teachable moment for giving them lifelong skills and creating lifelong clutter clearers.

Once a year, encourage them to go through their stuff, getting rid of old toys, old school supplies, games with missing or broken pieces, books they no longer read, clothes they've outgrown, unused electronics, and anything else they no longer use. Ask them when was the last time they played with it? Is it broken? Would they feel good letting another child enjoy it as much as they did now that they're done with it? Get them excited about the project by making it theirs.

MEMBER OF THE PACK

Helping out gives kids a sense of contributing and belonging to the family unit or tribe, not to mention confidence in their own capabilities and a sense of having something meaningful to offer. Kids can also be great at thinking outside the box and coming up with creative solutions to things like where to store extra boxes of cereal or the best place to leave their backpack so they'll remember it each day.

*Conversely, when kids offer to help out and the offer
is rejected, they start to doubt their capabilities or feel
they are not part of the group.*

Furthermore, researchers at La Trobe University in Australia found that kids who "do chores" develop better executive functioning, working memory, academic performance, and problem-solving skills.

Find ways to turn helping out time into together time by chatting about their day or what they hope to do this weekend while you get things done. Or make it fun by making it a game or a mini-party. Blast some tunes and dance around as you make an assembly line to put the groceries away or change the sheets on the bed. As an added note, while the tasks should be age-appropriate, experts suggest that you start introducing little tasks when they are just out of toddler stage. If you wait until they're older, the die will have been cast and you'll have a battle on your hands, with them either unused to helping out or, worse, feeling entitled and flat-out saying, "No."

Recognition can be its own reward. Sometimes just a "thank you" or a "good job" is enough to encourage kids to participate and let them know their contribution is valued. And while earning an allowance can help teach financial independence, beware of paying for everyday pitching in. A study by author Michaeleen Doucleff, Ph.D., (published in the book *Hunt, Gather, Parent*) suggested that bribing kids to pitch in, via a toy, a treat, or allowance, is actually counterproductive to them wanting to help out.

TOOLS AND THINGS

Literacy may be the most important skill anyone can have. If you can read, you can pretty much do anything. Starting kids early can set up a great habit for life.

The most creative thing I ever saw was a little nook my cousin Angie created in her son's room with bookshelves, a curtain, and a plush ottoman. Insanely adorable!

A book nook. Have you ever seen anything cuter?

What about the debris – the toy planes, trains, and automobiles, not to mention crayons, video games, plugs, etc.? When it comes to toddlers and their things, I have one word: plastics. That is, plastic bins where you can contain things like Lego® sets, plush toys, dolls, etc. Keep like things together in each bin and paste a photo on the front showing what goes in each. Even before they can read, the kids will know where to find what they want and where to put things back at the end of the day.

Once kids get past the toddler stage, a table (farmhouse style or desk) for arts and crafts, gaming, and homework becomes important. This is a good time to transition from plastic bins to baskets for storing art and craft supplies. A blackboard or a whiteboard might be a fun thing to add for spontaneous doodles or solving of math problems. Perhaps even a trunk for toys or costumes.

Another thing kids' rooms need are shelves for displaying mementos, keepsakes, collectibles (I had a stuffed mouse collection for years), recognitions and awards, and gifts from the grandparents.

Sports gear should have its own drawer, shelf, cabinet, or cubby to make sure everything is kept together and accessible.

CHEAP TRICK

When it comes to kids, they are growing and changing so quickly that you need to become a master curator – getting rid of things, toys, and clothes they no longer use and acquiring the new ones they want or need now.

But, the monetary costs for all those new things kids grow into needing can be overwhelming. Why not start a share group with family, friends, or other parents at your kids' school where you can donate items your kids no longer need and look for things they do? Additionally, there are lots of websites where you can sell, give away, or pick up all manner of items in your area.

13.

GUEST ROOM – LET THEM THINK THEY'RE STAYING AT THE RITZ

"Did you ever notice when you go to somebody else's house, you never quite feel a hundred percent at home? You know why? No room for your stuff. Somebody else's stuff is all over the goddamn place! And if you stay overnight, unexpectedly, they give you a little bedroom to sleep in...Right next to the bed there's usually a dresser or a bureau of some kind, and there's no room for your stuff on it. Somebody else's s*!t is on the dresser. Have you noticed that their stuff is s*!t and your s*!t is stuff? God! And you say, 'Get that s*!t off of there and let me put my stuff down!'"

George Carlin (American Comedian)

BE OUR GUEST

Friends and family play a hugely important role in our lives. They help define who we are and our place in the world. If we don't get a chance to see them very often, the times we do are all the more special. So, when they come to stay for holidays or a summer break it's a chance to connect and spend some quality time together.

But no matter how excited you are to see these folks, chances are you're going to run into at least one of two problems. First, where the heck do you put them? If you're one of the fortunate few, you have an available bedroom. For everyone else, guests mean rearranging the home office, bunking the kids together, or putting sheets on the couch.

The other concern is how long are they staying? Which can translate to: "And when did you say you were leaving?" Because no matter how much you love them, after a few days you might be screaming for your space and time back.

With those things in mind, here are a few ideas to make having overnight guests more fun, simple, and elegant, not to mention less stressful for all concerned. It can all be summed up in...

HOSPITALITY 101

I NEED MY SPACE

To make guests feel at ease, make sure they have room for their stuff. Clear surfaces and create space for them to put down not just their suitcase(s), but also wallets, purses, sunglasses, keys, phones, chargers, etc.

ELEGANT TIP

A suitcase stand is an inexpensive and super-elegant touch, and a great way for guests to store luggage with easy accessibility.

I NEED YOUR WI-FI

Make sure you've made a space for their laptop. I leave a computer pad down on the desk in my home office, as that room doubles as a guest room via a pullout sofa bed. More importantly, I leave them a note with the Wi-Fi network name and password. (If you really want to get fancy, you can type it up and even put it in a little frame.) Of course, it's the first thing anyone asks for.

CHEAP TRICK

Make your guests think they are staying at a five-star hotel. Place a carafe of water and some snacks in the room – nuts, fruit, and chocolates work well – along with utensils, plates, and napkins. If you really want to take it up a notch, surprise them with turndown service and a chocolate on the pillow.

ENTERTAIN ME

Leave out some books, magazines, playing cards, crossword puzzles, and the like. Your guests will be entertained, even through jet lag.

A guest room/office combination.

Other things you might want to consider leaving out for guests:

- Extra blanket and pillows
- Wastebasket
- Alarm clock
- Box of tissues
- Lamp on side table
- Empty hangers in closet and space to hang clothes
- Drawer space
- Accessible wall outlet
- Small fan/heater
- Pen and paper
- Fresh flowers

For the guest bath, helpful things to have on hand include:

- Bath towels, hand towels, and washcloths
- Toiletries – shampoo, conditioner, lotion, soap, toothpaste, toothbrush, feminine products, razors, etc. (If you're anything like me, you have a collection of sample and hotel amenity sizes.)
- Cleared space for their "stuff"
- Wastebasket

14.

HOME OFFICE – MAKING WORK FROM HOME WORK FOR YOU

"Allow the beauty around you to inspire your most soul-led authentic work."

Tara Marino (Founder, Elegant Femme /
elegantfemme.com, @elegantfemme1)

Since fateful March 2020, more and more of us are working from home, whether it's all of the time or part of the time. Which begs the question – exactly *where* do we work when working from home? If you have a dedicated office, lucky you for having the space. If not, what is doubling as your office? The coffee table? The kitchen counter? The dining room? No matter where you call the office, any way you can distinguish your workspace from the rest of your home (or room) is important. Bookshelves, room dividers, curtains, Japanese *shojis* (translucent so they diffuse rather than block out light), and screens help designate and separate spaces, allowing you to create a boundary between work and home.

Another way to separate work life from home life even when there's no commute? Remember to shut down your computer come quitting time. That sends a signal to both your brain and your body that the workday is officially over and it's time to live the rest of your life and recharge. (Bonus: this practice also extends the lifespan of your device and can improve its performance, as well.)

THE SETUP

You want your office, wherever it might be, to be an inspiring place you enjoy being. Adequate lighting is a must. Extra points if it's natural light. Open windows, when possible, help keep you and your ideas fresh. If you have an actual desk, it should be in what's called the "power" or "command" position in feng shui. That means facing, or at least able to see, the door. The idea is that if your back is to the door, you are subconsciously on alert, wary of anyone who might come up behind you. And anyone might, in fact, come up behind you.

Western lore has it that James Butler "Wild Bill" Hickok, a very fast and deadly gunslinger, was challenged so often that he always faced the door, especially when playing cards. Except once. For whatever reason, one day, while playing poker, he had his back to the tavern door. An unhappy player from the previous day walked in and shot Bill in the head from behind. He died immediately, *purportedly* holding what is now called the "dead man's hand" – a pair of black aces, a pair of black eights, and an unknown fifth card (per Wikipedia).

CHEAP TRICK – Dedicated Office

Go Ahead, Brag a Little

If you have a home office or work nook, save money and time on decorating. Fill walls and shelves with photos, letters, plaques, awards, newspaper clippings, etc. – things that highlight your accomplishments or adventures. Do not hide your light under a bushel. That said, don't overdo it. Creating a sense of whimsy with something like a gallery wall will show off your personality and keep things from looking dated.

"Me!"

NEATNESS COUNTS

A cluttered desk is both a symptom and a cause of a cluttered mind. A neat desk leads to improved focus, clearer thinking, better decision-making, more productivity, and less procrastination. It really does make a difference when things are straightened up, put away, and filed. Hanging folders, manila folders, drawer inserts, and in/out trays can all help contain the papers threatening to take over your desk – and your sanity.

When I was just starting out in the production world, I got a job on a TV special. I was young, naïve, and not at all pulled together. Wow, did I get a wake-up call! One night one of the senior producers took me out for a drink – and to let me have it. I was not doing a good job. The exact words included, "And I don't want to have to wait five minutes while you look for the piece of paper with the information I need."

I was reformed right there and then, vowing never to embarrass myself like that again. Sure, there've been lots of other embarrassments (too many to count), just not one exactly like that. In fact, at one of my next jobs, another producer left me a note, "Stop keeping your desk so clean. You're making the rest of us look bad."

ELEGANT TIP

Uplevel your workday. Drink your water from a wine glass. Keep a candle, diffuser, or flowers on your desk. Play music that inspires you.

FLOW WITH IT: THINGS THAT MAKE THINGS EASIER

Digital Clutter:

Even if you've got the physical clutter under control, don't forget about the digital stuff – the emails and texts you haven't dealt with, the 400 apps. of which you only use five. This stuff weighs on us as well. Half of it can probably be erased without even needing to deal with it. And don't neglect cleaning up your computer desktop. I once worked with someone who was being run ragged by all the projects he was overseeing. As a result, he must have had 100 folders on his laptop. I kept thinking a system of subfolders would make things more navigable. I got a headache just looking at it!

Office Supplies:

Just like having extra toothpaste in the bathroom, keeping extra office supplies on hand (copy paper, pens, pencils, post-its, staples, binders, notebooks, paperclips, and especially printer ink) helps keep you prepared and moving forward. Dedicate a drawer, cabinet, or shelf to these supplies – and to making life easier when you run out of something. If you have a supply of unused journals or notepads, you can even put them on a bookshelf and go "shopping" to find one you like each time you need one.

The Password Is…

I am totally smitten with this great – and cheap – organizer I found. A very small spiral-bound notebook, it's organized alphabetically and looks like an old-fashioned personal phonebook, but instead of spaces for names and numbers, it has spaces for the login and password for each site you use.

Watch Out for Those Wires:

Make sure you are not, literally and figuratively, tripping yourself up at work. Hide and/or wrap all cords. Get rid of cords and chargers you don't need. You may find you have duplicates or that many can pull double duty in more than one device.

CHEAP TRICK

I've already mentioned the blue light emitted from our devices, which can strain your eyes and mess with your sleep-wake cycle (circadian rhythm). You can block this blue light with a specialized screen protector (I have one on both my laptop and my phone), amber glasses, or clip-ons that fit on your existing glasses. And don't forget sunscreen – titanium dioxide and zinc oxide in the formula offer protection against the UV and high energy visible (blue) light emitted from your devices. Finally, check your devices for apps which reduce blue light (per linkedin.com). By using mineral sunscreen rather than chemical you skip things like possible carcinogens, hormone disruptors, and skin irritants that that may be hiding in the chemical SPF ingredients (per goop. com).

TIME MANAGEMENT

It's easy to buy into the idea of "not enough hours in the day" or the need to hustle (which I, personally, am no longer here for). The good news is that studies have shown that longer hours don't necessarily equal more productivity, meaning it is possible to achieve more while doing less. With a few practical and mental tweaks, you may be able to shift your mindset and open up more time than you thought possible.

Step one is making sure you are living congruently with what you say are your priorities, making room for what matters and filtering out the rest.

A few specific tips to help you manage your time:

- Cancel a plan. Open up space on your calendar.
- Similarly - just say no. Stop feeling so obligated to respond to every non-urgent and unimportant email, watch every video you get forwarded, or accept every invitation you are offered. No explanation necessary.
- Time is our most precious commodity, so guard yours jealously. No one knows how much time they've got, but one thing's for sure, they aren't making any more of it. Be intentional about what you say yes to. Respect your own boundaries around time, remembering that when you save part of your time for yourself, you're saving part of your energy for things that matter to you.
- Become a one-touch manager by only dealing with an issue once, whether it's a piece of paper, email, text, or phone call. See it. Respond to it. Be done with it. When you can quickly and decisively handle the question, issue, or decision without any sense of resistance, why not have it done and dusted? However, there are times when procrastination or a feeling of resistance is a message. If it feels uneasy or forced, by all means, take that as a sign that now is not, in fact, the time to act.
- If you want to commit to a project, cross out days and times on your calendar in advance as a reminder not to schedule anything then.

- When working on a large project, something creative, or when you're on a hard deadline, close emails and turn off notifications. Those small disruptions and temptations eat into more time than any of us may realize.
- 80/20. The 80/20 Rule (mentioned earlier in connection with clothing) has a work corollary: 20% of your effort nets you 80% of your results. This begs the questions: Are there some things you're doing that really don't have to be done? Which aren't getting you enough results to justify the time spent doing them? Or are you in a position to delegate certain tasks?
- Should you really "eat the frog" first? Eating the frog first is the concept of doing the largest, hardest, most unpleasant task first, before moving on to easier, more pleasant or mundane things. In other words, get it over with. I disagree with this philosophy and here's why: Chances are, you have a long to-do list. Many tasks may be tedious, but they are relatively quick and easy to do (call the vendor, pay bills, send out a meeting invitation, etc.). So, I suggest getting those out of the way first. That way, when it comes to eating the frog (a truly unfortunate phrase), you're not feeling the weight and distraction of the twelve other things you need to get done and can actually concentrate on the frog...so to speak. That said, really consider whether you need to eat the frog at all. Is this something that actually needs to get done? Will it truly net you results? Is there an easier way to go about getting it done (such as breaking it up into chunks)? Better yet, can you delegate it?

All of the above being said, I would add that most of us spend the majority of our time dealing with the "urgent" (timely, what we think needs to get handled right now) rather than the "important" (that which will advance or support our business, career, lives). Don't lose sight of, or put off, the important because you are too busy doing the urgent. My father, who led an exceptionally varied and fascinating life, was always going to write his memoir once everything on the "urgent" list (the emails, calls, organizing the garage or the photo albums) was handled. Everything else was never handled. It never is. There will always be a list of things calling for our attention. Sadly, my father passed away having written only the smallest part of his book.

So many of us wear our struggle, hustle, capability, and to-do lists as badges of honor – often to the point where they become our identity, our measure of our worth. Hand raised. I used to feel the need to be the first to arrive, last to leave work every day. I no longer feel the need to measure myself in this way. And the funniest thing has happened – I am actually much better, calmer, and more effective at whatever I'm doing.

While I think more and more people are considering, or reconsidering, the space work occupies in their lives, the hustle-to-prove-your-worth mentality is deeply ingrained in our culture. When my stepfather died, three men spoke at his funeral. What struck me was how each of them talked about his accomplishments (and there were many) and none of them talked about *him*. That made me sad.

MEANING...?

As humans, we have the need for meaning and service in our lives. While we can certainly find those in myriad ways and places, finding them in our daily work can be truly rewarding and fulfilling. Yet some of us have become so burnt out after years on a treadmill that doesn't light us up that we've lost sight of what does.

If you, like so many over the past few years, have been reevaluating what holds meaning for you and haven't homed in on anything, try imagining specifics:

- Most importantly, how do you want to spend your time?
- What gives you a sense of service?
- Where do you imagine yourself geographically?
- Who are you serving? Are people buying your crafts online? Do you help couples on the brink of divorce?
- What type of environment are you in? Office? Home? Beach? Film studio?
- What are you wearing? Suit? Shorts and T-shirt?
- Are you traveling? Where?

Thinking about these kinds of things may give you an idea that surprises you. And if you find that idea a bit intimidating, or if you think it's already been done, remember you are the only one who brings to it your unique set of talents and experiences.

15.

KITCHEN – CURATION AND STORAGE FOR LESS OVERWHELM

"Everything happens in the kitchen – life happens in the kitchen."

Andrew Zimmern
(American Culinary Expert and TV Personality)

HOW DO I LOVE THEE? LET ME COUNT THE WAYS

We finally get to my favorite room in the house – the kitchen. And I'm not alone. Anecdotal – and realtor – evidence shows that the kitchen is one of the two most important rooms influencing a buyer's decision whether or not to purchase a house (the other being the primary bathroom).

That's because the kitchen is where everyone seems to gather. It's where we share confidences over coffee and cookies. It's where we make new memories and recreate old ones, like making Mom's potatoes au gratin.

On the face of it, the kitchen is about cooking. But it goes so far beyond that. For the cook, making food is personal. It may be a way to unwind after a full day, as it is for my brother, Michael. It may be a way to express your creativity, trying out new pairings and techniques. It may be a way to show love and to nurture. It may be all of these things.

No matter how you view or define it, the kitchen is a huge part of what makes a house a home. It's where the magic happens, where the disparate veggies, fruits, boxes, and cans get made into fantastic, yummy meals to be shared with loved ones.

Food has the power to warm you on a snowy day. It can transport you to another place, like Japan, India, or France. It can get you to take time out to connect with someone you care about or want to get to know better.

OK, by now you may have guessed I sort of like food. Especially Italian food.

It all started in Rome, at Alfredo's, home to the famous fettuccini dish. I was maybe eleven years old when I discovered Alfredo and his creamy, gooey goodness. Sometime after we got home my mother opened an Italian restaurant in Los Angeles. By then I was so in love with the pasta with the cream, butter, and cheese sauce that the dish was actually listed on the menu as Fettuccini Maria.

$$\rightarrow Paste \leftarrow$$

Penne Arrabbiata	11.^{00}
Linguine alle Vongole	16.^{00}
Fettuccine Maria	14.^{00}
Spaghetti alla Checca	12.^{00}
Tagliatelle Bolognese	22.^{00}

Who needs Alfredo when you've got Maria?

This love of food has followed me into the professional world. In my TV production life, I have worked tangentially on a few cooking programs, which translated to me often watching cooking shows all day long. Viewing culinary porn for hours? Heaven! So much so that I signed up for cooking classes. Thanks, Chef Eric.

And if you don't see yourself as a cook but think you're ready to test the waters? The best way to get started, the gateway drug to chefdom, is a good knife or set of knives.

IT'S ALL ABOUT THE LOVE

Years ago, my amazing friend Becky took me to a restaurant in Denver run by Hare Krishnas. The fare was simple and vegetarian, yet there was something so incredible about it. I couldn't put my finger on it, but everything tasted – and felt – amazing. Becky let me in on the secret ingredient: *prasadam* (or *prasada*), a Hindu concept which literally means "mercy" from Krishna, but often refers to food which has been prepared with love and offered to Krishna before anyone else enjoys it (per krishna.org). In other words, what I was tasting – and feeling – was lots of intentional love sent to the food.

A similar concept in Arabic, called *nafas*, translates to "breath" or "spirit." Cooks with *nafas* are said to produce better food than those without, even when using the same recipe.

Of course, if you don't want anyone copying your recipe, *nafas* or not, you could try what my grandmother did. My stepmother (The best ever! Amazing! Adore her!) had asked her for the recipe for her Mexican breakfast crepes with cinnamon, which we kids all loved. They came out OK, but not quite like Mama Dee's. Well, one day my stepmom got up early and caught good ole Dee in the act – of adding beer to the batter, an ingredient she'd managed to "forget" when sharing the recipe.

The concepts of *prasadam and nafas* aren't nearly as "woo-woo" as they may sound. People who pray over food are offering gratitude, also a form of love.

ELEGANT TIP

Whether you're cooking for a group, a party, or even dinner for one, don't forget presentation. Plating is just restaurant speak for how things look when served. Whether it's a fruit plate, a charcuterie board, a bowl of soup, or steamed vegetables, little touches like a sprig of parsley, a wedge of lemon, or arranging avocado slices in a fan shape can make food look elegant and irresistible. We eat with our eyes first.

WE GATHER TOGETHER

The kitchen is where people naturally congregate. Whether it's family after a full day or an entire party of friends, everyone just seems to end up there. It's the hub of the house where moments and memories are created.

Since everyone inevitably ends up in the kitchen, especially at a party, keep things simple:

- Remember the snacks. Put out bowls of nuts, olives, crudité, chips, and dips…whatever people can easily grab and munch.
- Enlist help. Give everyone a job. Put someone on wine duty (uncorking, pouring), have someone else grating cheese, another chopping garlic. They'll appreciate having something to do and the chance to contribute. (Note: This may push your control freak buttons. Breathe. It's OK if someone does something slightly differently than you. Test your ability to go with the flow and receive support.)

THE ORGANIZATION'S THE THING

The kitchen is a place where a lot of stuff just seems to end up. It's home to piled up mail, junk drawers full of things you can't identify (bits and bobs you found on the floor not knowing where they came from), takeout menus and packets of ketchup, soy sauce, etc., toys your pet no longer plays with, even eyeglasses with no known owner (maybe a guest from months ago who never called to claim them?).

Do I need to say it?

Curate. Curate. Curate.

Go through the mail, keep unidentified objects corralled in a small container if you're too afraid to toss them yet. Takeout menus are doubtless online. Takeout packets are highly unlikely to get used. Whittle down the number of pet toys. And those eyeglasses may benefit someone if donated (some optometrists accept them). You get the picture.

While you're at it, go through old plastic bottles, plastic utensils, chopsticks, mugs, and bags of all sorts. Check storage containers to see if they are cracked or broken and that every top has a bottom and vice versa. Figure out what gets used, is usable, and is worthy of keeping.

Once you've had a good cleanout, you may be inspired to upgrade your storage, being sure to leave surfaces with enough clear space to prep and cook.

The number one way to make a kitchen look organized and elegant is to keep the counters clear.

I'm a believer in keeping storage areas like pantries and cupboards hidden behind solid cabinet doors. It makes the space feel less cluttered than storage with no doors or glass doors.

Finally, consider "building up," creating as much vertical storage as possible. For example, wire shelving units for the cupboard or pantry essentially turn one level into two by offering storage space on top of and underneath the unit.

Food storage – if you can't see it, you can't find it. If you can't find it, you won't eat it. I cannot tell you how much food in my house went bad because I'd forgotten about it and didn't see it in the back of the refrigerator. Or how many times I bought duplicates of fridge and pantry items because I didn't know we already had them, thus creating more clutter.

Bins, baskets, and canisters are all great ways to corral, store, and display food. I'm a big fan of storing dry goods (buy in bulk and ditch the packaging) such as legumes, grains, and pasta in glass canisters or jars. Those can then be labeled to note what's in each one – a huge help when trying to distinguish between brown rice and quinoa or mung beans and lentils. To make sure things are eaten while still fresh, you can add the purchase date when labeling.

Not mine. I wish!

CHEAP TRICK

If you're undertaking a major kitchen organization project, edit first. By getting rid of anything out of date and consolidating like products (rice, pasta, etc.) you will free up space. After the edit comes the organization, including landing on an organizational system and buying any needed supplies, such as the aforementioned bins, baskets, and canisters. But edit first so you don't buy anything you don't actually need or too much of what you do.

ELEGANT TIP

Take off produce stickers from things like bananas, onions, apples, oranges, avocados, etc. as you unpack groceries. It's simple and makes things look a bit more elegant, especially if they are stored in a basket on the counter.

CHEAP TRICK

When scraping anything off a cutting board, use the back of the knife and save wear and tear on both the knife and the board.

OUT OF DATE

According to Recycle Track Systems (rts.com), in the United States we discard thirty percent of the entire U.S. food supply, often because of unclear expiration labeling. "Sell by," "use by," and "best before" can all be confusing. This translates to food taking up more space in U.S. landfills than anything else. Feeding America says that 108 billion pounds of food are thrown away (wasted) each year, when we take into consideration factors like:

- Uneaten food from homes, restaurants, and markets
- Crops left in fields because of low crop prices or too much of the same crop
- Problems with the manufacturing and transportation of food
- Food not meeting retailers' standards for color and appearance

Some ways to combat food waste at home include:

- Making – and sticking to – a list before shopping.
- Not overbuying at the market (so things get eaten before going bad).
- Wash produce as soon as you get home. It will make it easier, and thus more likely, for it to get used (remember activation energy).
- Keeping things visible in the refrigerator.
- Storing and displaying like things together. In the fridge this means an assigned area for meats, one for leftovers, vegetables, dairy, etc. In the pantry, keep all grains and pasta in one place, with other sections for beans, sauces, and the like. For the freezer, this means keeping all ice cream in one place, frozen veggies in another, and so on.
- Label Items. 'Nuff said.
- Using every bit of every item – for instance, vegetable scraps make great stocks and sauces.
- Similarly, turn any extra food into soup. Everything from avocados to leeks, lentils, and asparagus can be made into a light or hearty addition to any meal.
- Freezing individual portions of fruit such as strawberries and bananas for smoothies.

CHEAP TRICK

Not sure what to do with leftovers? Reheat and add an egg or two. Scrambled, fried, poached, jammy, or hardboiled, eggs give life to any leftover – be it Italian, Chinese, or Indian. Perfect for an easy breakfast.

ELEGANT TIP

This one also happens to be a Cheap Trick. If you ever see cookware (such as Pyrex® or CorningWare®) at a great price (garage sale, flea market, bargain bin), buy a few sets. That way, when you take a dish to a potluck or family gathering, you won't worry or care about taking it home – you can leave it with your hosts.

IT DON'T MEAN A THING IF IT AIN'T GOT THAT ZING

Nothing flavors up a dish more than the right spice, or combination thereof.

THE GOOD NEWS

Not only do spices add flavor to dishes, but according to health.com, each of the staples in our rack or on our shelf comes with its own health benefits, such as improving digestion (turmeric), controlling blood sugar (cinnamon), or antioxidant and anti-inflammatory properties (cumin), to mention just a few. You can get the most flavor out of jarred spices by heating them in oil or a dry pan before adding to food.

THE BAD NEWS

Spices don't stay fresh forever. Store them away from sunlight and heat, not next to the stove. Buy in the smallest quantity possible. Better to replace more often than have to toss out something that is doing zip to give your dishes zing.

Spices are the spice of life.

FENG SHUI AND THE STOVE

The stove not only represents nourishment, in feng shui it also represents fire energy, affecting abundance and wellbeing in every area of your life. So, keep your stove maintained and clean. Rotating the use of the burners is said to activate opportunities and abundance from a variety of sources.

MORE GOOD JUJU

A few other tips for creating good karma – and good health – for yourself and the planet:

Buying organic (or even regenerative or biodynamically produced, which take things a step further) fruits, vegetables, bread, sauces, and pasta cuts down not only on the number of pesticides you're exposed to, but the amount of pesticides released into the atmosphere and water from "conventional" farming. Furthermore, farming practices that use pesticides expose growers, pickers, and other handlers to increased levels of toxins.

Buying local produce, which is easy to do if you have a weekly farmer's market in your area, supports local growers, ensures the food is fresh and in season (which equals more nutritional value), and cuts down on the carbon footprint associated with transporting food (and all goods, really) over long distances.

Eating fruits and vegetables that are in season has one more advantage – they "mimic" what your body is asking for in any given season – cooler and lighter in the warmer months, warmer and heartier in winter.

Another Earth-friendly habit to adopt is composting, and it's easier than you may think. If you have a compost bin you can throw in your scraps of uncooked fruits and veggies ("green bits"), along with a bit of old flowers, yard clippings, and leaves ("brown bits"). Just remember no bones or protein (including meat, fish, and dairy). It takes several months for this mixture to turn into beautiful, rich soil, so some people have two bins (if they have the space) and alternate adding scraps to one while the other is left to develop into dirt. They also make countertop composting machines that will convert small batches of scraps into potting soil within a couple of hours.

On the other hand, if you don't have a compost bin, you may be able to throw your fruit and veggie scraps into your yard clippings trash bin, if your area uses those and allows it. Certain areas have companies that will pick up your compost and deliver a clean bin weekly.

Finally, if you have no other way to compost, check with your local farmer's market. Many accept bags of compostables. Just store everything in a bag (or bags) in the freezer until you're ready for a farmer's market run.

No matter how you do it, composting reduces what gets sent to the landfill and the amount of CO2 that stuff gives off, plus when added to soil, compost helps draw down carbon from the air.

A special note about my love – coffee. Used grounds can easily be composted or, if you have a garden, they make great mulch for water-loving plants (it helps the soil retain moisture) such as Hibiscus, Iris, and Lily of the Valley (per wellandgood.com).

Additionally, banana peels and water can be put in a blender to make plant food that improves the PH and potassium levels of soil.

FRIENDLY SWAPS

According to the Environmental Protection Agency, Americans generate almost five pounds of trash each day. Each. Much of this comes from the kitchen. While huge changes are needed on global and systemic levels to deal with this issue, we all can take responsibility to do our small part.

> *"Reduce. Reuse. Recycle." We've all heard this famous mantra. By limiting the number of items that make it into your home, especially the single-use ones, you're saving money and helping to save the planet.*

There are lots of easy, eco-friendly swaps we can all make if we haven't already:

- Reusable shopping bags
- Biodegradable trash bags (including for cleaning up after your pets)
- Reusable water bottles
- Reusable straws (I love my glass ones. You can also buy stainless steel ones)
- Use rags instead of paper towels
- Biodegradable sponges
- Tea in a biodegradable bag (many aren't) or loose leaves
- Coffee made in a French press or brewing with a reusable filter or refillable pods

PLASTICS: JUST SAY NO

Of all the things that make it into our kitchens, the worst environmental offender is plastic. Unsurprisingly, Reuters reports that the U.S. produces more plastic waste per capita than any other country. Most plastics are made from petrochemicals. From production to disposal, there is a huge environmental cost in terms of toxic emissions. Plastic also takes hundreds of years to break down, and both the production and breakdown of plastics result in microplastics. These tiny particles have been found in the air we breathe, not to mention in food (especially seafood) and drink, from which they make their way into the human body, potentially causing oxidative stress (*Science of the Total Environment*).

Most plastic is not recycled, or even recyclable, and ends up in landfills or one of the world's five ocean garbage patches.

DO YOU "WISHCYCLE"?

Many of us rinse our plastic bottles and packaging, put them in the bin, and hope they actually get recycled.

The information on recyclability is confusing. Most plastic containers have a number within the three-arrowed triangle at the bottom. This number is meant to reflect the exact kind of plastic used and whether it is recyclable. But there is contradictory information about which numbers are recyclable and which are not, and the mere existence of the arrow does not mean the item can or will be recycled. Much of the plastic sent to be recycled ends up in landfills, anyway, because it is not clean and dry.

Indeed, wishcycling your plastic can backfire and cause problems for the recycling facility, which may choose to send *everything* to the landfill if unrecyclable plastics are found mixed in with recyclable items. So it's best not to buy plastic in the first place.

CLEAN GREEN

Cleaning is another place where you can just say no to toxins. There are lots of natural dishwashing soaps, glass cleaners, tub scrubs, and other cleaning products on the market. None, however, is as versatile as white vinegar, which I swear has seemingly thousands of uses and can replace a multitude of toxic cleaning products. Specifically, mindbodygreen.com notes that using natural cleansers such as vinegar in the kitchen keeps you away from things like surfactants (which can cause breathing issues and irritate skin), solvents (which can cause shortness of breath and skin or eye irritation), and fake fragrances (whose components are not required to be divulged as they are considered proprietary, and may include allergens, hormone disruptors, and chemicals which may harm the nervous system).

So, if you want to just say no to all of these toxins, say yes to white vinegar instead.

- Diluted in water it makes a great cleaner for glass and metal.
- Sprayed onto a paste of baking soda and water, it makes a great cleaner for pretty much any sealed and non-porous surface.

When *not* to use vinegar:

- Do not use vinegar on granite countertops – it can etch the surface, making it look cloudy.
- Do not use vinegar on aluminum surfaces, including certain stainless steel utensils (knives, forks, spoons), as it can stain (per mindbodygreen.com).

THE KITCHEN IS CLOSED

If your house is anything like mine, the kitchen never seems to close, except after dinner. That's a great time to make sure everything is cleaned, put away, and ready to go in the morning. I like to wash all dishes, pots, and pans and put them in the dishwasher or, for things that get hand washed, back in the cupboard. You can also wipe down the stove, countertops, and fridge and mop or sweep the floor. The whole thing should only take around fifteen minutes tops. Waking up to a clean kitchen, ready to go for the day, is so worth it.

TOTAL GARBAGE

Running the disposal, if you have one, can be included as part of shutting down the kitchen. Read the manual and make sure you only "feed" it things it can handle. (Different makes and models can tackle different items.) If your disposal ever gets temperamental, it also helps to keep a disposal wrench on hand to reset it. All of which is to say, you want to treat your disposal kindly if you want to keep it in working order.

Here are some tips to do just that:

- Never put anything but food down the disposal.
- Never run the disposal without also running cold water (helps keep grease solidified). Continue running the water for a short bit after you turn off the disposal to keep pushing things through the pipes.
- No stringy food like celery, artichoke, or banana.
- No bones.
- No large amounts of fat (especially bacon fat), which can congeal and clog pipes, including those of your local sewage system.
- Lemon and lime wedges can make a sink smell nice if your disposal can handle them. Squirt a little extra dishwashing liquid in at the end if it can't.
- Keep your fingers away from a running disposal. That little rubber guard is there for a reason. (You'd think this would go without saying, but you'd be surprised.)

16.

DINING ROOM – CREATING CONNECTIONS THROUGH FOOD

"For me, the dining room is the most important room in the house. Why? The dining room is where the dining table is. The dining table is where the food is. Where there's food, there's love."

Constance Towers (Actress and Singer)

Sobremesa is a Spanish tradition or term referring to the time you spend at the table after you've finished eating.

While *sobremesa* directly translates to "over the table," it really has to do with the time spent after eating, continuing the conversation with friends and family.

I love the idea of *sobremesa* because not only do I love food, I love the idea of honoring mealtime, of honoring what we eat, how we eat it, and who we eat it with.

MR. MANNERS IS UNDER THE TABLE

Dinah Shore was an actress, singer, and talk show host back in the day. She loved to cook – even published a few cookbooks. My father knew her and when we were very young (and I stress *very*), he'd take my sister and me to Dinah's house for dinner. Sometimes it would be just the four of us. To make things fun, and to make sure my sister and I behaved, she would tell us that Mr. Manners was hiding under the table and keeping an eye on us. We kept looking under the table for him. And giggling. And giggling. We loved the attention and the game. And, of course, we behaved like perfect angels.

Food and dining are synonymous with moments of connection. Like having dinner with Dinah Shore – and Mr. Manners – some of our best memories are made around the table when we share a meal with people we love. After all, the dinner table is where we come together at the end of a full day, unwinding over food, drink, and company.

The Blue Zones® show us that real-life social networks play an important role in our health and longevity. So, when we fill up on bonding as well as food, we're supporting our overall wellbeing beyond that one meal. Win-Win!

And while Mr. Manners may not be hiding under your table (he's still very busy with me), there are certain things you can do to make mealtime more simple, easy, elegant, and engaging for everyone, starting with...

ANYBODY SEEN A TABLE AROUND HERE?

Just like the entryway, the dining table seems to be where a whole bunch of stuff ends up – mail, papers, computers – especially if it doubles as a desk for you or your kids. You may even be shoving things to the side in order to eat, which I'm willing to bet ends up making mealtime more rushed and less relaxed, even if you don't feel it consciously. Or, if you have a nook or counter where dinner seems to happen, the dining table may rarely get used for actual dining, allowing you the "luxury" of not paying attention to the built-up piles.

Even if the dining room is not the most used room in your house, a table covered with so much stuff that you have to sweep things to the side just to find the actual table underneath is not doing you any favors. To create more ease and flow, devise a system for dealing in a timely manner with the things that tend to pile up there. Make sure everyone in the household knows what this system is. Coats, hats, etc. should go in a closet or on hooks in a mudroom or entryway. Kids' backpacks should go in their rooms. Papers and mail should be dealt with, filed, or tossed. It may help to get a few "inboxes" where active work and homework projects can be kept.

In addition to the table begging to be cluttered, er decluttered, dining rooms often have pieces that store things like real silver, special china, tablecloths, trivets for under hot dishes, etc. In my experience, these cabinets tend to be black holes, housing…you have absolutely no idea what. This is definitely a place where you want to take everything out, sorting through it to determine what you actually like, what you actually use, and what is actually usable (read: not bent, broken, or chipped). Put back only what you love, what you use, and what fits with a fresh perspective and inventory knowledge. Ditch the rest.

ELEGANT TIP

Use your best dishes and silverware. Don't save your best things for special occasions only. Your life is being lived now. You're here now. Enjoy your nice things now.

IMPORTANCE OF MEALTIME

Life is full of so many pleasures. Hiking. Apple picking. Seeing your favorite team win the big game. These experiences help us live life to its most joyful fullest. But so often the *need* for pleasure (and it absolutely is a need) goes unrecognized or undervalued.

While there can be sensual pleasure from eating an orange over the sink, I'm an advocate of elevating the pleasure of a meal even if it's a meal for one. A single flower in a bud vase is not only beautiful, it reflects elegance and self-care. If you're dining with family or friends and want to take it a step further, you can have fun putting together a tablescape that is vintage, seasonal, modern, shabby chic, or whatever. Even a bowl of fruit and some green leaves can kick things up a notch.

Did you know that how you eat matters as much to your health as what you eat?

Isn't eating different when you're stressed out versus when you're calm and relaxed? The fact is, true health is connected to how we experience our meals.

So, stop and make time not just to eat, but to dine. For years I held a full-time day job and a part-time night job. I would have a snack in between, usually in the car while driving, but I always saved dinner until I got home, even though that was almost midnight. I guess I'm a Spaniard at heart. I didn't want to miss out on a decent meal and *sobremesa* – even if it was just with myself.

A few other tips to honor yourself, the people you're eating with, and the food you have taken the time to prepare:

- Elbows off the table (old fashion etiquette tip).

- Phones put away.

- No discussing exercise or diet.

- If it's just you and your partner, try not talking about money, work, schedules, or kids; see what you come up with to discuss and find out about each other.

- Be aware of eating too fast, rushing to the next thing.

CHEAP TRICKS

If you have a family, you can make mealtime simpler by:

- Giving everyone a job, like setting the silverware or getting out the napkins.

- If you have little kids, give them crayons and put down butcher paper (two layers to protect the table surface) or placemats that can be sponged off and reused.

- Consider keeping utensils in buckets (one for forks, one for knives, one for spoons) and letting everyone grab what they need. This gives off an easy, beachy, family feel.

- Leave out a Lazy Susan with everything on it – oil, salt, pepper, condiments, whatever you use on a regular basis.

- A mini-whiteboard or chalkboard can be a fun way to announce the "menu" for the evening.

THE SETTING

Some rules are made to be broken. And sometimes it's good to know the rules even if you're gonna break 'em.

Whether you're going for a casual, formal, or themed table, a basic setting – one that is Mr. Manners approved (well, Emily Post and the like) – applies pretty much across the board. Of course, even these tips may be a bit formal for your everyday:

- Start with putting down placemats, tablecloth, or runner.
- Next place the dinner plate.
- The salad plate goes on top of the dinner plate if you're serving salad first.
- If you're serving soup first, the bowl goes on top of the dinner plate (and on top of the salad plate if you're serving soup before salad).
- If you're putting out a bread-and-butter plate, the plate goes above and to the left of the dinner plate.
- Napkins go on top of the dinner or salad plate or to the left of the dinner plate, underneath or to the left of the fork(s).
- Glasses go to the upper right of each place setting.

Flatware gets arranged in the order of use, from the outside in, like this:

- Forks on the left of the mat or plate, with the smallest (salad fork) on the outside working in toward the plate.
- Knives go to the right of the plate, with the one to be used first (if there is more than one) on the outside.
- Spoons to the right of the knives, working from the largest on the outside to the smallest on the inside.

- Dessert spoon and fork go at the top – horizontally above the placemat or plate. The handle of the fork points to the left. The spoon goes above the fork with its handle pointing to the right.
- The butter knife goes on the bread plate with the handle facing in toward the diner.

A beautiful table setting – not by yours truly.

> ### ELEGANT TIP
> B is for…
>
> Here's a super-simple way to remember which bread plate and which glass(es) are yours at the table. Also super easy to teach kids:
>
> - Make the okay sign with both of your hands. This turns your left hand into a lowercase "b" and your right hand into a lowercase "d." Wait for it…bread goes to the left side (your hand making the "b") and drinks go to the right side (your hand making the "d").

For more formal occasions:

- Charge it: Consider using a charger, a large plate that is either taken away right before serving or left as a base upon which you can put other dinnerware (plates and bowls).
- If you're having a large and formal party you can designate where everyone should sit by putting a place card right above the dessert utensils.
- If everyone is getting their own salt and pepper shakers (*très élégant*), those will bookend the place card, salt on the left and pepper on the right.
- If you're feeling particularly fancy, you can even make menu cards announcing the fare for each course.
- While I've never served oysters (though I've eaten my fair share), if you are game, please note that the oyster fork actually goes to the right of the dinner plate, the exception to the rule of forks on the left.

- Napkin rings look elegant and special. You can even wrap the utensils inside the napkin if the ring will fit over it.
- If you happen to have starched napkins on hand, you can play with folding them into different shapes. (Hello, Mr. Swan.) I got to try this when I took a napkin folding class on a cruise ship. But you don't have to buy a ticket on the high seas, check out YouTube for tutorials.
- When it comes to glasses, they get placed in the order of which wine you will be serving with each course, starting with the wine glass closest to the water glass (to the left of all glasses) and working out.

When it comes to giving your table a "look," AKA tablescaping:

- Keep all centerpieces low. Be it a bowl of fruit or a vase of flowers, a centerpiece should not block anyone's view of anyone else. When keeping it low, you can decorate the table from one end to the other as long as things aren't feeling too crowded.
- If you want to create some visual interest, try building your place settings "up." Stacking chargers, dinner plates, and napkins, one on top of the other, offers a sense of texture.

THE SERVICE

You probably won't worry about this on a daily basis, but for formal table service:

- Food gets served from the left of the person being served.
- Liquids, including soup, get served from the right.
- Dishes get cleared from the right (sans stacking).

ELEGANT TIP

To uplevel your serving game for special occasions:

Chill salad plates in the freezer

Warm dinner plates in the oven (yours may even have a warming drawer or setting)

Though most wine doesn't need to be decanted, serving red wine from a decanter ups its flavor profile and looks particularly elegant

TIME TO PARTY

When it comes to party planning, keep just a few things in mind.

Never Keep 'Em Guessing: Obviously, you want to let guests know what kind of a party you're throwing and how to dress – formal, casual, garden, holiday-themed. Something I picked up in Ireland which I think works really well is letting guests know the parameters for cocktail hour. For example "7:00 for 8:00" means 7:00 p.m. cocktails and 8:00 p.m. dinner. People can arrive anywhere within that one-hour window. Personally, I think forty-five minutes is about the max to stretch cocktails. After an hour guests will be getting tipsy from drink and faint from hunger.

One thing not to invite to dinner is overhead lighting at the table. It does nobody any favors. Candles, and even lamps, are less harsh and cast a softer glow.

Taking pictures and posting photos of your soirée may sound like a good idea, but I have my reservations. When people put down their phones they are more engaged in the moment and their memories of the evening will be better and truer than anything a snap could capture.

Depending on the kind of celebration you're throwing, a great solution can be to create a designated photo area. Set up a corner with wigs, hats, glasses, etc., and let everyone go to town there. Makes the photos fun and special.

In the end, the most important part of entertaining is the atmosphere you set. If you are relaxed and having fun, your guests will be too.

ELEGANT TIPS

- Plan any games, music, and activities in advance, reducing last-minute stress.
- Unless they are newly dating, seat couples separately (even at different tables if you have more than one). They will get to connect with other people and then have lots to talk (make that gossip) about on the way home.

SETTING THE MOOD

My mother was a wonderful hostess and cook. Her second husband loved being able to bring home a group of people for dinner... unannounced. She always managed to effortlessly and graciously throw something together. Well, one night he brought about six people home, but good ole mother's cupboards were bare. All she had on hand were canned pea soup and hotdogs. Still, she set a gorgeous table in the formal dining room and people could not stop commenting how this was the best pea soup and hotdogs they'd ever had. Great food? Doubt it. More like proof of what a few candles and nice dishes can do.

ELEGANT TIPS

When you're the guest at the party, never arrive empty-handed. A bouquet of flowers, a plant, or a bottle of wine or sparkling water all do the trick nicely. The next day it is nice to call, text, or email to say thanks.

17.

LAUNDRY AND MUDROOM – OUT, DAMNED SPOT!

"Laundry Room – loads of fun."

As seen on Etsy

My great friend Teresa swears I do more laundry than anyone else – ever! She's convinced I must be taking in other people's wash. To set the record, and Teresa, straight – not true, not true, not true. In fact, every time I do laundry I kind of think, "Well, that's done," as if I won't have to do it again in ten days (which is actually how long I tend to go).

Laundry areas and mudrooms are often the most neglected spaces in the house. So, it's time to show them a little love and perk things up. No reason we can't make them, as I keep saying, intentional, functional (practicality rules here), inviting (at least to you), and, yes, even beautiful. No reason we can't make them a place you won't mind hanging out – at least for as long as it takes to fold the clothes. No reason we can't make them a place that is not screaming "chores" at you. Of course, if you don't have a designated laundry room, this may not apply to you.

If you do have a dedicated laundry room, step one is to decorate and make it look finished. What would make the space seem cheerful to you? A sunny color of paint? A whimsical bouquet of large, wooden flowers?

CHEAP TRICK

When it comes to decorating, this is a great place to hang and frame some childhood artwork – either yours or your kids'.

Once you've got the place looking good, start thinking in terms of setup, keeping it streamlined to a few basics.

THE BARE NECESSITIES: STORAGE AND MORE

- Shelving/cupboards for laundry supplies
- Sink for hand washables or soaking
- Bins, cubbies, or baskets for miscellaneous items like wayward single socks, clothes waiting for stain removal (though it's best to do this as early as possible) or mending
- Hook or place for iron and ironing board, or standing or handheld steamer

THE BARE NECESSITIES: SUPPLIES

- Stain remover
- Detergent (perhaps one for colors, one for whites, and a special lingerie cleaner)
- Bleach or bleach alternative (many are more eco-friendly)
- Reusable wool dryer balls are less toxic and more eco-friendly than dryer sheets. The lanolin from the wool also helps cut down on static cling. I keep mine in the dryer so they don't take up any real estate on the shelf.
- Hanging rod/line and/or metal folding racks for things that don't go in the dryer
- Mending supplies – buttons, threads, and needles (Note: I save all extra buttons that come with new clothes separated into baggies by color and all stored in a plastic bin. You could also repurpose a smallish toolbox.)
- Suede, leather, and shoe cleaner/polish

Making the most out of a small space.

A NOTE ON STAIN REMOVAL

I can create a stain better than just about anyone. My sister Cristina, on the other hand, can get *rid* of stains better than just about anyone (she calls it her "crap superpower"), so she gets to work her magic on practically all my clothes.

Here are a few of her hints on stain removal:

- For liquid stains, blot first.
- Use stain removers along with a soft brush (such as a toothbrush) with which you can gently scrub the stain. This loosens the fabric's hold on the stain.
- Stubborn stains may require soaking.
- Oil or grease stains? Use dishwashing liquid or, believe it or not, automotive degreaser.
- Sea salt, soda water, and baking soda work great for red wine stains.
- Specialty products are best for ink or coffee, but in a pinch, you can try hairspray or rubbing alcohol for ink and a paste of oxygen bleach and water for coffee.

CLOTHES TIME

When I was young my mother had a friend who was a very high-society lady. And I lucked out – she gave me one of her silk blouses. A navy blue V-neck, short-sleeve pullover, I thought it was quite sophisticated and wore it right away. Then into the laundry basket it went. Fate would have it that my mom came into my room and grabbed everything in the basket to throw in the laundry, including the blouse. What I got back was fit for a rag doll rather than me. When asked why the shirt had gone into the washer and dryer (it really needed to be dry cleaned), my mother responded that she hadn't imagined I owned anything so nice. Really, lady?! Now that I'm older and have more than one nice thing in my wardrobe, I am very careful about how I care for – and separate – my clothes.

Speaking of which…did you know there is a debate over how often to wash your clothes? Some people, including Stella McCartney, recommend washing your clothes as infrequently as possible. As long as they're not full of stains or too offensive, the idea is to save wear and tear on what you wear. In fact, Anderson Cooper says he rarely washes the jeans he wears nearly every day, and when he does, it's by wearing them in the shower. Personally, I go the other way. If I wear it, I wash it. Of course, the chance of me getting through a day without getting some sort of gunk all over my clothes is pretty slim. My father always used to say that I looked good in everything I ate. (Is that nice?)

That said, please note that synthetic fiber fabrics like polyester love to hold onto oil from the skin, which can contribute to body odor. Natural fibers tend to hold onto odor less and, thus, need less washing. Wool especially locks away the icky stuff (per *The Washington Post*).

No matter how often you do, or don't, wash your clothes, remember that most clothes and detergents do just fine in cold water, thus dramatically reducing the amount of energy you use and the amount of money you pay for it. In fact, *The Washington Post* reports that water heating consumes about ninety percent of the energy used to run a washing machine, as well as emitting large amounts of $CO2$ into the atmosphere. You can also save lots of energy, as well as wear on the fabric, by airdrying.

- Everything Inside Out: Turn everything inside out before washing. The easiest way to do this is to turn them inside out before you throw them in the hamper, so they'll be good to go straight into the washer.

- No More Tangles: To avoid things getting tangled in the washer, tie all drawstrings on sweatpants, pajama bottoms, and pants. Even better, put them in net bags. (I always tie the string when I hang them up, as well. Makes for a neater closet.)

- Zip it: Leave all zippers zipped (they won't corrode or rust as easily and it keeps them from rubbing against other garments, thus damaging them).

- Not So Buttoned Up: Leaving all buttons unbuttoned means less strain on buttons – and less need to sew them back on. It also means less strain is exerted on buttonholes, preventing them from stretching.

- Fabrics: Certain rough fabrics, like towels, can be abrasive to more delicate fabrics, like t-shirts, accelerating wear and tear on the item. Be sure to separate loads accordingly.

- Overstuffed: It is possible to overfill the washer, meaning clothes won't get as clean as they normally would. If your machine is a top-loader, you can also burn out the motor with a load that's too big or unbalanced.

CHEAP TRICK

It's a tale as old as time. The inevitable sock getting lost somewhere in the wash-dry process. One safeguard against this is to pin socks together with a safety pin when you put them in the hamper. You can wash and dry them and they'll never spend a moment apart. There are also special washing machine net bags for socks.

(ODD) ELEGANT TIP

I find that towels and sheets often smell like vinegar when new. (I have no idea why.) Always wash them before first use.

REMOVE PROMPTLY

- Remove clothes promptly from washer: Clothes start to smell if left wet for too long.
- Remove them promptly from dryer: Cuts down on wrinkles.

ELEGANT TIP

Washing lingerie and other delicate items in net bags saves on the need to hand wash.

CHEAP TRICK

Putting a dry towel in the dryer with wet clothes not only cuts down on drying time, your clothes come out fluffier.

CHEAP TRICKS

Caring For Your Washer

- Regularly run an empty load with concentrated laundry soap or a special detergent made for cleaning the washer.
- Many washers have a filter that should regularly be cleaned out – check your owner's manual.

Caring For Your Dryer

- Clean out the lint trap after every load. Your clothes will dry faster and built-up lint can become a fire hazard.
- Regularly clean out the lint from the vent hose and vent (you can buy special brushes for this).

Final thought: The better organized and streamlined your laundry room is, the faster you can get out of it and enjoy the rest of your life!

THE MUDROOM

Full disclosure: I've never actually lived in a place with a mudroom. I remember the first time I saw one, at my friend Becky's house in Northern California. At first I was surprised, then a bit confused. Then I became impressed by how useful the whole idea was. A special place to drop coats, boots, umbrellas, and backpacks? Clever thinking, that.

Except...for so many mudrooms, "drop" seems to be the operative word, as in everything gets strewn everywhere.

A few items to help give everything its own place:

- Canvas bags, bins, or baskets to hold miscellaneous items
- Hooks, pegs, or racks for coats and backpacks
- Boot scraper (to stop you from tracking mud through your house)
- Seating, such as a wooden bench, for taking off boots
- Shoe rack for both outdoor and indoor shoes
- Umbrella stand

18.

GARAGE – SHOULDN'T IT BE A PLACE TO PARK CARS?

"Almost 1 in 4 Americans say their garage is too cluttered to fit their car."

Survey from Gladiator® GarageWorks

The poor, humble garage – nobody shows it any love.

Dictionary.com defines a garage as "a building or indoor area for parking or storing motor vehicles."

It does not define a garage as "a place where you store all your things to the point of being unable to park a motor vehicle in it."

Yep, the American garage, home to tools, old books, bikes (often unused), workout gear (also often unused), old furniture (frequently inherited with no plan for where it might go), washing machines, extra refrigerators, and boxes of memorabilia. But rarely home to cars.

In other words, the garage is a place where a whole lot of stuff tends to end up, often with the idea of "for now." But "for now" tends to become "forever." And as more and more things end up there "for now," more and more things end up piling up "forever." This can continue to the point where you don't even know what it is that you're storing (you've totally forgotten), or you don't really care about or use what's in there because you no longer need it.

If this sounds at all familiar, it's time for an honest, thoughtful clearout:

- Start, as always, by taking everything out of the area.
- Return anything that doesn't belong in the garage to its proper home.
- Now decide what you're putting back.

When was the last time you went inline skating? Do you need two picnic baskets? What are you getting out of that stash of mementos from high school? Seriously consider what holds value for you (sentimental and monetary) and what actually serves your life now.

By taking this kind of inventory, you can free both physical and emotional space (old objects hold old energy, and not always in a good way) and, perhaps, make room for your car, thus protecting its exterior and guarding against theft. After all, your car is likely your biggest or second-biggest investment, depending on if you rent or own. Why park it outside in order to store a bunch of stuff you don't need, use, or love?

So what can you sell, donate, repurpose, or trash?

Once you've done your clearout, you'll want a system for organizing everything you've kept.

Think about creating zones for household items, lawn chairs, sports gear, etc. Hooks, wall racks, overhead storage racks, magnetized rails for tools, bins, and pegboards all work great to corral wayward stuff.

A dedicated shelf for seasonal decorations is a great way to keep those things in one place. A clear-front hardware organizer with drawers for things like screws, bolts, and nails is very helpful any time I'm trying to DIY something (admittedly, not that often). As much as possible, stay vertical with storage. There are even companies that can design shelves that hang from the ceiling for you.

My father and stepmom came up with a genius way for their garage to double as a gym without giving up parking in it. Simply back the cars into the driveway, move a few pieces of equipment into place, and get to working out. Stow equipment and return cars to garage when done.

Turning your garage (or any space in your home) into a place to work out means you don't have to travel to the gym or pay for a membership!

CHEAP TRICK

Use your imagination to add a bit of personality to an otherwise drab space. School pennants, kids' artwork, caricatures from visits to theme parks, and posters are all inexpensive and personal ways to add a pop of fun and color to the garage.

ELEGANT TIP

Always Have Something On Hand

Create a (re)gifting section for holding presents. Whether in a garage or elsewhere, a gift area (a place that also has ribbons, gift bags, wrapping paper, and cards) can be a time and mind saver when you need to pull off a last-minute gift (hostess, birthday, graduation, etc.).

19.

TRAVEL – SIMPLICITY AND ELEGANCE ON THE GO

"Adventure is worthwhile in itself."

Amelia Earhart

(20th Century American Aviation Pioneer and Author)

This may seem to be going far afield, but it's really not that far. And yet, it's as far as you want to go. I'm talking about travel.

Because, while it's not part of the home, if you ask me, travel is an essential part of living and growing. I have such a hunger for experiencing new cultures, sights, adventures, and food. Mostly the food.

The thing is, we need to curate our travel the way we curate our homes. By which I mean being intentional about where we go and what we take with us. Because you don't want to make the mistake of taking the clutter with you in the form of too many toiletries, clothes, books, and papers. More on that in a minute.

First…

WHERE ARE YOU HEADED?

I have a game I play. I love to ask people, "Where do you want to travel or visit? What calls to you about that place?" I love hearing their answers and am always a bit surprised when they have to stop and think about it.

I can tell you two of mine. The first is Italy – specifically Tuscany. Though I've been there briefly, I would love to go back for an extended time, especially Florence. I just imagine soaking up the warm sun, strolling the charming piazzas, meeting welcoming and boisterous people, and visiting the nearby vineyards. I want to taste lemons, espresso, and bread dipped in peppery olive oil, all while seated next to people who are loud and warm and passionate, people who live fully and emotively.

I also want to visit Bali, to explore the temples, do yoga, bathe in blessed waters, and eat gorgeous plant-based meals.

Every good trip starts with a Bloody Mary.

"NO" BEFORE YOU GO

As mentioned, you don't want to be taking the clutter with you to Fiji. To that end, I offer you a few of my most simple and elegant travel tips:

NO NEED TO PACK MAKEUP OR TOILETRY KITS

I love this tip. I never have to pack makeup or toiletry kits. Ever. That's because I always keep a bag of toiletries and one of makeup packed and ready to go. These can be filled with samples, gifts with purchase, or things you're about to run out of which still have a few uses in them. Obviously, this won't apply to you if you only get on a plane or take a road trip once every three years, but I can tell you it has certainly served me well, in good times and bad – like when I was driving to Santa Barbara from Los Angeles every weekend when my mom and stepdad were both very ill.

NO NEED TO OVERPACK

No overpacking. This starts with choosing a color theme. Tan with navy. Black and red. Green and various shades of blue. Things that mix and match easily and can be used for multiple occasions. This gives you a great chance to pair things you haven't thought of before. But the real genius part is that it cuts down on the number of shoes you need to pack since you're not trying to match so many different colors. And shoes are bulky, heavy, and take up a lot of room, let me tell you.

This is a lesson I learned the hard way: Barcelona, Spain, many years ago. I decided (because why wouldn't I?) that I'd pack all kinds of cute clothes and shoes (oh my, the number of shoes!) for a quick jaunt to the Ciudad Condal from Paris. Thing is, because I hadn't stuck to a color theme, I ended up with one heavy bag – and one large problem.

Long story short, we had one day to explore the city before heading elsewhere. Ready to check my bag at a locker or hold station at the train depot, I soon discovered there was no longer such a place for luggage due to terrorist threats. Toting the damn thing all over town was not going to work. (I swear it weighed more than I did!) So, my sister and I ended up stuck for about ten hours in the train station, which, I might add, did not have very good food. Thank goodness I got a do-over in Barcelona years later. It does, in fact, have very good (world-famous) food.

Even if you've done a great job packing light, it doesn't mean you have to carry on. I'm a fan of checking baggage. The long walk to security and the gate is so much easier and quicker without having to schlepp anything, while overhead bins tend to be crowded and hard to reach (at least for me). Nowadays, many airlines charge a fee for both carry-on and checked bags for most tickets, so I think checking bags is worth it to eliminate the abovementioned hassles. And it really doesn't take all that long to get your bag from the carousel.

How to pack: Always choose a bag – from the smallest purse to the largest suitcase – that has compartments in it.

I love being able to categorize and separate my things. When it comes to packing clothes, many people (including myself) are fans of rolling rather than folding. It offers up just a bit more space and cuts down just a bit on wrinkles.

NO OVERDOING THE BOOKS AND PAPERS

Physical books and papers take up a lot of space and add a lot of weight to your luggage. Be intentional about what you are taking and what you will actually get to. Some people feel vacation will give them the time to go through stacks of paper and reading material. But, if you haven't gone through that stack of papers in a month, I can pretty much guarantee lugging it to Tokyo won't make it any more likely to happen. You'll be too busy visiting the fish market, Skytree tower, and tea houses.

ENJOY THE RIDE

Here are a few things I *do* carry onto the plane with me.

- Eye mask
- Socks
- Chargers
- Books (digital or physical), magazines
- Sweater or shawl
- Noise-canceling headphones (these not only help preserve your hearing, but you have no idea how much calmer you feel without that low-level cabin noise, which can cause a surprising amount of subconscious anxiety)
- Cross-body purse, backpack placed across the front, or belly pack facing the front, all with zippered compartments – anything that makes a pickpocket's job that much harder.

What I don't wear on the plane is jewelry. I pack it in my carryon, but I don't like to wear it. There's too much chance of losing it going through security (where you have to take it off) or on the plane, like the earring I lost because I fell asleep and it fell off into the seat. By the time I noticed, I'd already gotten my bag and was waiting for my ride.

BAREFACED

I don't like to wear makeup on airplanes. The cabin environment is harsh and dry and can end up encouraging thirsty skin to drink up anything it can, thus clogging pores. However, since the air is so dry, I do always moisturize, moisturize, moisturize beforehand. A tinted moisturizer works great to offer a little bit of coverage.

SUNSCREEN IS A MUST

Per thepointsguy.com., if you're cruising at 30,000 feet you are about six miles closer to the sun than when you are on the ground. Airplane windows are made from materials that filter out most UVB rays. However, an open cabin window shade will expose you to lots of UVA rays, especially if you have a window seat. Those UVA rays contribute to sunspots, wrinkling, and skin cancer. So put on that sunscreen before stepping on the plane. Pull down the shade if you're in a window seat and can bear missing any flyover sights.

ELEGANT TIP

Consider your choice of travel/airplane wear. While it doesn't have to be formal by any stretch, you may not be doing yourself any favors by going too casual. I once got upgraded to First Class from Los Angeles to London because I showed up at the check-in desk not fancy but at least pulled together. I won't lie – that eleven-hour flight was much better because of it. Wide-leg pants with a roomy middle, loose shirt, closed-toe flats, and a cardigan is a nice, comfy outfit that makes sprinting through terminals as easy as possible. Additionally, I always suggest dressing for the climate on the plane and not for the weather of where you're departing or arriving. Layering is always a great option.

CHEAP TRICK

Are you familiar with plane-itis? Planes are notorious spreaders of all manner of bugs, mostly due to the questionable recirculated air. Plane-itis is the sinus infection you catch from breathing in all that sketchy oxygen. Furthermore, if what you've caught is viral, it won't respond to antibiotics the way bacteria do.

Well, here's a way to never catch plane-itis again: When on a plane, keep your neck and chest completely covered and warm. Wrap a scarf around your neck, chest, and shoulders. If you can at all stand it, turn the air vent over your head way down or even off. Toasty – and works like a charm. I was introduced to this by a doctor and have not had a case of plane-itis since. It's worth noting that most planes have significantly upgraded their filtration systems, but plane-itis is still very much a thing.

Paris is always a good idea (with Colleen).

WHEN TRAVELLING INTERNATIONALLY

- Make sure you have an international power adapter for the regions you'll be visiting. I have one that is usable for any country (at least it hasn't failed me yet).
- Make sure your credit card doesn't charge foreign transaction fees. If it does, get a new one for the trip.
- Verify that your credit card can be replaced internationally if it gets lost or stolen – with a new card sent to your hotel or your bank's/institution's local office.
- Be aware of any roaming fees you may incur from your cellphone carrier. If you don't have an international plan, you may be able to pre-purchase a package that offers substantial savings.

ONCE THERE – WHEREVER THERE IS

- Be a gracious guest, respectful of the culture, traditions, people, and laws. I truly believe that I am a guest in any town, city, or country I visit and try to behave as such.
- Stretch your comfort zone. Absent safety concerns, don't be afraid to get adventurous and head off the tourist-beaten path. My friend Christina and I ended up spending one trip exploring the jungles outside Cancún, navigating the backroads to Chichen Itza, and learning to SCUBA dive through a shipwreck in Cozumel.
- I always get at least one souvenir from wherever I've been. Something that catches my eye and makes me smile. It doesn't have to be expensive by any means. I just like having something to remember my travels by.

Finally, the one thing I've learned from my travels is that we all, we humans, have so much more in common than we do differences. We all want the same things: wellbeing, community, love, security, and a home to return to – decluttered or not.

"Dès Vu – the awareness that this will become a memory."

Urban Dictionary

20.

Action List – How To Start Decluttering

"If you understand that space truly equals infinite potential and opportunity, then you get that stuff in that space limits it."

Karen Rauch Carter (Feng Shui Consultant and Healthy
Lifestyle Designer / karenrauchcarter.com)

First, consider why you need to declutter:

- What is making any given space feel "cluttered"?
- What is the energy in the room? Heavy? Stagnant?
- How does it make you feel? Drained? Uninspired?

- What physical items are causing that energy and feeling?
  - Too many things on flat surfaces?
  - Too much furniture?
  - Furniture which could be rearranged to create a clearer path?

Out:

- Start slow and small – no need to tackle anything overwhelming right off the bat.
- Empty each drawer, shelf, cabinet, etc. completely before tackling the items in it.
- Clean it.
- Decide what goes – use boxes to designate what gets donated, what gets (re)gifted, what gets sold.

In:

- Shop what you own – what can you repurpose and use elsewhere?
- Put back only what you are called to keep – what fits the space, your taste, and your lifestyle now.

Finally, create an organizational system, buying only what you need to maximize the space and look of what you are keeping:

- Could you use some plastic shoe boxes?
- Shelf dividers?
- Hooks?
- Drawer organizers?

- Bins, baskets, canisters, and a good label maker are invaluable tools for creating an organizational system that is functional and sustainable.
- For everything that isn't stored in a closet, cupboard, or drawer, get creative and have fun displaying your treasures on shelves, tables, and walls.

Be prepared – once you get started, you're going to see potential and beauty within your home, and in your own decluttering skills, that you never saw before.

"The best time to plant a tree was 20 years ago. The second best time is now."

Proverb of Unknown Origin

21.

THANKS FOR STOPPING BY

"The pain of parting is nothing to the joy of meeting again."

Charles Dickens (English Writer and Social Critic)

We humans are actually hardwired for ease, order, and beauty, whatever our own definitions of those are.

I hope you can use the tips, tricks, and information in this book as inspiration to create your own unique vision of your home – and yourself – in the world.

> *Remember, our lives and our homes are constantly evolving. We will never be done.*
> *The goal is progress, not perfection.*

It is such an honor to even imagine someone reading this book. Thank you.

Until we meet again, in whatever format, I wish you simplicity and elegance – and so much love.

"In the end, only three things matter: how much you loved, how gently you lived, and how gracefully you let go of things not meant for you."

Gautama Buddha (Religious Teacher)

ACKNOWLEDGMENTS

With so many people to thank, I barely know where to start. I have so much appreciation for every person on this list.

Tara Marino of elegantfemme.com. You gave me both the inspiration and courage to write this. The work we've done together has not just changed my life - it has helped create my life.

Lori Elgin, for your unwavering support and insistence on acknowledging and celebrating wins big and small, I will forever be in your debt and your Maruchi.

Cristina Gavin, for all your creative input, copy editing, and photo editing. Even more for being my sister, sounding board, and savior, always. There are no words.

To the following people who I am humbled to call friends and family (listed alphabetically): Chiqui Bianco, Lawrence Biscontini, Katie Bleifer Jones, Teresa Cebrian, Connie Gavin (where would I be without you?), Cecilia Gonzalez-Andrieu, Julia Hodes, Nancy Sunkin, Colleen Quinn, and Amber Weekes. Thank you so much for your unending love, support, and input.

And thank you to everyone at the Awakened School and Deep Pacific Press:

- Datta Groover for the creative advice
- Rachael Jayne Groover for the practical advice
- Jennifer Snowball for her incredible organization and fielding much more than her fair share of emails
- Karen Collyer for the amazing amount of editing, truly incredible
- Amy Salvage

And, lastly, Grammarly.

I love you all.

Works Cited

All Great Quotes. *"Oscar Wilde Quotes."*
Accessed February 24, 2023.
https://www.allgreatquotes.com/picture-of-dorian-gray-quotes-58/

American Academy of Sleep Medicine. 2015. *"People at risk of hoarding disorder may have serious complaints about sleep."* ScienceDaily, 8 June 2015.
www.sciencedaily.com/releases/2015/06/150608213030.htm

Antipolis, Sophia. 2021. *"Bedtime Linked With Heart Health."* European Society of Cardiology, November 9, 2021.
https://www.escardio.org/The-ESC/Press-Office/Press-releases/Bedtime-linked-with-heart-health

AZ Quotes. *"Quotes. Author. O. Oscar Wilde."*
Accessed February 24, 2023.
https://www.azquotes.com/quote/891562

AZ Quotes. *"Quotes. Author. W. Wayne Dyer."*
Accessed February 25, 2023.
https://www.azquotes.com/quote/867590

Baylor University. 2018. *"Can Writing Your 'To-Do's' Help You to Doze? Baylor Study Suggests Jotting Down Tasks Can Speed the Trip to Dreamland."* Baylor University, January 11, 2018. https://www.baylor.edu/mediacommunications/news.php?action=story&story=192388

Brainy Quote. *"Amelia Earhart Quotes."* Accessed February 26, 2023. https://www.brainyquote.com/quotes/amelia_earhart_130007

Brainy Quote. *"Andrew Zimmern Quotes."* Accessed February 25, 2023. https://www.brainyquote.com/quotes/andrew_zimmern_926424

Brainy Quote. *"Charles Lamb Quotes."* Accessed February 24, 2023. https://www.brainyquote.com/quotes/charles_lamb_119227

Brainy Quote. *"Confucius Quotes."* Accessed February 24, 2023. https://www.brainyquote.com/quotes/confucius_104254

Brainy Quote. *"Dream World Quotes."* Accessed January 19, 2023. https://www.brainyquote.com/quotes/juan_felipe_herrera_724359?src=t_dream_world

Brainy Quote. *"John Burroughs Quotes."* Accessed February 24, 2023. https://www.brainyquote.com/quotes/john_burroughs_106918

Brainy Quote. *"Maria Mitchell Quotes."*
Accessed February 25, 2023.
https://www.brainyquote.com/quotes/maria_mitchell_317076

Brainy Quote. *"Max Eastman Quotes."*
Accessed February 24, 2023.
https://www.brainyquote.com/quotes/max_eastman_107843

Brainy Quote. *"Vladimir Nabokov Quotes."*
Accessed February 24, 2023.
https://www.brainyquote.com/quotes/vladimir_
nabokov_385288

Breus, Michael J. 2021. *"The Four Chronotypes: Which One Are You?"*
Psychology Today.
April 10, 2021.
https://www.psychologytoday.com/us/blog/sleep-
newzzz/202104/the-four-chronotypes-which-one-are-you

Cambridge Dictionary. *"Curation."*
Accessed February 24, 2023. https://dictionary.cambridge.org/
us/dictionary/english/curation

Cambridge Dictionary. *"Simplicity."*
Accessed February 27, 2023.
https://dictionary.cambridge.org/dictionary/english/simplicity

Cameron, Donna. *"A Year of Living Kindly."*
January 10, 2017.
https://ayearoflivingkindly.com/2017/01/10/where-is-your-querencia

Chiu, Allyson. 2022. *"Why You Should Almost Always Wash Your Clothes On Cold."* Washington Post, November 29, 2022. https://www.washingtonpost.com/climate-solutions/2022/11/29/laundry-cold-water-environment/

Christie, Brendan. 2021. *"Nancy Glass on Her ProdCo's First 20 Years."* Realscreen, September 16, 2021. https://realscreen.com/2021/09/16/nancy-glass-on-her-prodcos-first-20-years-when-youre-happy-youre-more-creative

Cleveland Clinic, 2021. *"Are Cold Showers Good for You?"* Cleveland Clinic, June 17, 2021. https://health.clevelandclinic.org/are-cold-showers-good-for-you/

Dictionary.com. *"Garage."* Accessed March 23, 2023. https://www.dictionary.com/browse/garage

Doucleff, Michaeleen, PhD. 2021. *Hunt, Gather, Parent: What Ancient Cultures Can Teach Us About the Lost Art of Raising Happy, Helpful Little Humans.* United States: Avid Reader Press.

Environmental Protection Agency. 2022. *"National Overview: Facts and Figures on Materials, Wastes, and Recycling."* July 31, 2022. https://www.epa.gov/facts-and-figures-about-materials-waste-and-recycling/national-overview-facts-and-figures-materials#Generation

Erickson, Mandy. 2020. *"Setting Your Biological Clock, Reducing Stress While Sheltering In Place."* Scopeblog.stanford.edu, June 3, 2020. https://scopeblog.stanford.edu/2020/06/03/setting-your-biological-clock-reducing-stress-while-sheltering-in-place/

Feeding America. *"How We Fight Food Waste in the US."* Accessed November 12, 2022. https://www.feedingamerica.org/our-work/reduce-food-waste

Fetell Lee, Ingrid. *"3 Questions To Ask Yourself When Your House Doesn't Feel Like A Home."* Accessed February 25, 2022. https://aestheticsofjoy.com/2022/02/04/what-to-do-when-your-house-doesnt-feel-like-a-home/

Fetell Lee, Ingrid. *"Fix Your Home's Funky Energy With These 3 Tips."* Accessed March 4, 2022. https://aestheticsofjoy.com/2022/03/04/fix-your-homes-funky-energy-with-these-3-tips/

Fetell Lee, Ingrid. *"What To Do When You Don't See Eye To Eye On Home Design."* Accessed February 12, 2022. https://aestheticsofjoy.com/2022/02/11/what-to-do-when-you-dont-see-eye-to-eye-on-design

Fried, Carla. 2020. *"38 Billion Yearly on Self-storage: Better Spent on Retirement Savings?"* Rate, January 22, 2020. https://www.rate.com/research/news/self-storage-retirement-savings

Gaines, Joanna. 2018. *Homebody: A Guide to Creating Spaces You Never Want to Leave*. New York: Harper Design.

Genius. *"A Place for My Stuff."* Accessed January 17, 2023. https://genius.com/George-carlin-a-place-for-my-stuff-lyrics

Gerken, Tom. 2018. *"Tsundoku: The art of buying books and never reading them."* BBC News. July 29, 2018. https://www.bbc.com/news/world-44981013

Godfrey-June, Jean. 2023. *"Mineral versus Chemical Sunscreens: Understanding the Difference."* goop. July 25, 2023. https://goop.com/beauty/skin/mineral-versus-chemical-sunscreen

Good Reads. *"Gautama Buddha. Quotes. Quotable Quote."* Accessed February 26, 2023. https://www.goodreads.com/quotes/3181192-in-the-end-only-three-things-matter-how-much-you

Good Reads. *"Charles Dickens. Quotes. Quotable Quote."* Accessed February 26, 2023. https://www.goodreads.com/quotes/317780-the-pain-of-parting-is-nothing-to-the-joy-of

Good Reads. *"Jules Feiffer. Quotes. Quotable Quote."* Accessed May 1, 2023. https://www.goodreads.com/author/quotes/5116.Jules_Feiffer

Good Reads. *"Rumi. Quotes. Quotable Quote."* Accessed February 24, 2023. https://www.goodreads.com/quotes/35461-let-the-beauty-we-love-be-what-we-there

Harris, Tonya. 2021. *"A Homemade Degreaser Recipe + 3 Ways To Tailor It To Any Mess."* mindbodygreen, April 10, 2021. https://www.mindbodygreen.com/articles/homemade-degreaser

Huffington, Arianna. 2017. *The Sleep Revolution: Transforming Your Life, One Night at a Time.* United Kingdom: WH Allen.

Huffington, Arianna. 2021. *"The 7-Day Plan That'll Make a Nightly Ritual Out of Your Transition to Sleep Mode."* Well+Good, January 10, 2021. https://www.wellandgood.com/transition-to-sleep/

Kassis, Reem. 2021. *"Do You Have Nafas, the Elusive Gift That Makes Food Taste Better?"* The New York Times, April 1, 2021.

Krishna.org. 2022. *"Prasadam - What it is and why we should not eat anything else."* November 8, 2022 https://krishna.org/prasadam-what-is-it-and-why-we-should-not-eat-anything-else/

Kumar, Nanda. 2021. *"Should You Wear Sunscreen In Front Of Your Computer?"* LinkedIn, June 1, 2021 https://www.linkedin.com/pulse/should-you-wear-sunscreen-front-your-computer-nanda-kumar

La Trobe University. 2014. *"Children's Chores Improve Brain Function."* La Trobe University, June 14, 2022. https://www.latrobe.edu.au/news/articles/2022/release/childrens-chores-improve-brain-function

Lao XQ, Liu X, Deng HB, Chan TC, Ho KF, Wang F, Vermeulen R, Tam T, Wong MCS, Tse LA, Chang LY, Yeoh EK. 2018. *"Sleep Quality, Sleep Duration, and the Risk of Coronary Heart Disease: A Prospective Cohort Study With 60,586 Adults."* J Clin Sleep Med. 2018 Jan 15;14(1):109-117. doi: 10.5664/jcsm.6894. PMID: 29198294; PMCID: PMC5734879

Laurence, Emily. 2023. *"Your Starter Guide To What Plants Like Coffee Grounds - And The Best Ways To Use Them."* June 15, 2023. https://www.wellandgood.com/use-coffee-grounds-in-plants/

Lippe-McGraw, Jodi. 2018. *"Why You Should Always Wear Sunscreen on a Plane."* The Points Guy, November 8, 2018. https://thepointsguy.com/guide/why-you-should-wear-sunscreen-on-a-plane/

Lockett, Eleesha. 2019. *"Grounding: Exploring Earthing Science and The Benefits Behind It."* Healthline, August 30, 2019. https://www.healthline.com/health/grounding

Loewe, Emma. 2022. *"Why White Noise Doesn't Actually Help You Sleep + What To Listen To Instead."* Mindbodygreen, February 8, 2022. https://www.mindbodygreen.com/articles/white-noise-vs-pink-noise

Louisiana Department of Health and Hospitals. *"What You Should Know About Mothballs."* Accessed February 20, 2002. https://ldh.la.gov/assets/oph/Center-EH/envepi/Pest/Documents/Mothball_Fact_Sheet.pdf

Merriam-Webster. *"Beauty."* Accessed January 15, 2023. https://www.merriam-webster.com/dictionary/beauty

Merriam-Webster. *"Clutter."* Accessed February 24, 2023. https://www.merriam-webster.com/dictionary/clutter

National Alliance To End Homelessness. 2022. *"State of Homelessness: 2022 Edition."* https://endhomelessness.org/homelessness-in-america/homelessness-statistics/state-of-homelessness/

Noyed, Daniel. 2022. *"Weighted Blanket Benefits."* Sleep Foundation, updated March 11, 2022. https://www.sleepfoundation.org/bedding-information/weighted-blanket-benefits

Nunez, Kristen. 2022. *"Should You Be Drinking Water First Thing In The Morning?"* Real Simple, June 30, 2022. https://www.realsimple.com/health/preventative-health/benefits-of-drinking-water-in-morning

Oprah.com. *"Peter Walsh's Best Organizing Advice."*
Accessed February 24, 2023.
https://www.oprah.com/shiftyourlife/peter-walshs-best-organizing-advice_1

PR Newswire. 2015. *"Almost 1 in 4 Americans Say Their Garage is Too Cluttered to Fit Their Car."* June 9, 2015.
https://www.prnewswire.com/news-releases/almost-1-in-4-americans-say-their-garage-is-too-cluttered-to-fit-their-car-300096246.html

PR Newswire. 2015. *"Survey Finds 54 Percent Of Americans Are Overwhelmed With Clutter and Don't Know What To Do With It."* January 13, 2015.
https://www.prnewswire.com/news-releases/survey-finds-54-percent-of-americans-are-overwhelmed-with-clutter-and-dont-know-what-to-do-with-it-300019518.html

Quote Fancy. *"Peter Walsh Quotes."*
Accessed February 24, 2023.
https://quotefancy.com/quote/2123057/Peter-Walsh-What-I-know-for-sure-is-that-when-you-declutter-whether-it-s-on-your-home

Quote Fancy. *"Robert Southey Quotes."*
Accessed February 24, 2021.
https://quotefancy.com/quote/1422412/Robert-Southey-There-is-a-magic-in-that-little-world-home-it-is-a-mystic-circle-that

Quote Fancy. *"Stacy London Quotes."* Accessed February 25, 2023. https://quotefancy.com/quote/1301038/Stacy-London-Your-closet-needs-to-be-a-place-of-joy-and-celebration-of-who-are-you-now

Rahman A, Sarkar A, Yadav OP, Achari G, Slobodnik J. 2021. *"Potential Human Health Risks Due to Environmental Exposure to Nano- and Microplastics and Knowledge Gaps: A Scoping Review."* Sci Total Environ. (Science of the Total Environment), Feb 25, 2021. 757:143872. doi: 10.1016/j.scitotenv.2020.143872. Epub 2020 Dec 3. PMID: 33310568.

Reach for Montessori. *"Why Montessori Activities are Called Work."* Accessed February 28, 2023. https://reachformontessori.com/why-montessori-activities-are-called-work/

Reuters. 2021. *"Malaysia Sends Back Over 300 Containers of Illicit Plastic Waste."* Reuters Staff, April 6, 2021. https://www.reuters.com/article/us-malaysia-environment-plastic/malaysia-sends-back-over-300-containers-of-illicit-plastic-waste-idUSKBN2BT1YT

Robbins, Mel. 2021. *The High 5 Habit.* Carlsbad, CA: Hay House Inc.

RTS. 2022. *"Food Waste in America 2022: Statistics + Facts."* https://www.rts.com/resources/guides/food-waste-america/

Schwartz, Marnie. 2021. *"The Spice Is Right."* Health.com, April 2021.
https://www.pressreader.com/usa/health-
usa/20210401/281565178495927

Urban Dictionary. *"Bedgasm."*
Accessed February 25, 2023.
https://www.urbandictionary.com/define.php?term=bedgasm

Urban Dictionary. *"Dés vu."*
Accessed February 26, 2023.
https://www.urbandictionary.com/define.php?term=dès%20vu

US History. *"The Eclectic Ben Franklin."*
Accessed March 14, 2023
https://www.ushistory.org/franklin/autobiography/page40.htm

Vartan, Starre. 2021. *"'Sobremesa': An Untranslatable Spanish Delight."*
Treehugger. Updated August 19, 2021.
https://www.treehugger.com/sobremesa-an-untranslatable-
spanish-delight-4868600

Vocabulary.com. *"Simplicity."*
Accessed February 24. 2023.
https://www.vocabulary.com/dictionary/simplicity

Wikipedia.com. *"Dead Man's Hand."*
Accessed March 14, 2023.
https://en.wikipedia.org/wiki/Dead_man%27s_hand

Wikipedia. *"Elegance."*
Accessed February 24, 2023.
https://en.wikipedia.org/wiki/Elegance

Wikipedia. *"Querencia."*
Accessed April 10, 2023.
https://en.wikipedia.org/wiki/Querencia

Zoma. *"Who's Getting The Most Sleep?"*
Accessed 25 February 2022.
https://zomasleep.com/blog/whos-getting-the-most-sleep

Photo Credits

ABOUT THE AUTHOR

When she's not busy trying to make things simpler and more elegant, Maria Gavin is an Emmy award-winning producer and writer of unscripted and lifestyle television. She also teaches film and TV production at the college level.

A native of Los Angeles, Maria is passionate about food, travel, and adventure. She has a Master Chef certificate and is a certified SCUBA diver. She has also flown a plane and done a solo skydive – once each.

She likes to think she's funny. Please do not disillusion her.

Photograph: Don Hajicek